UNCLAIMED

HATJE
CANTZ

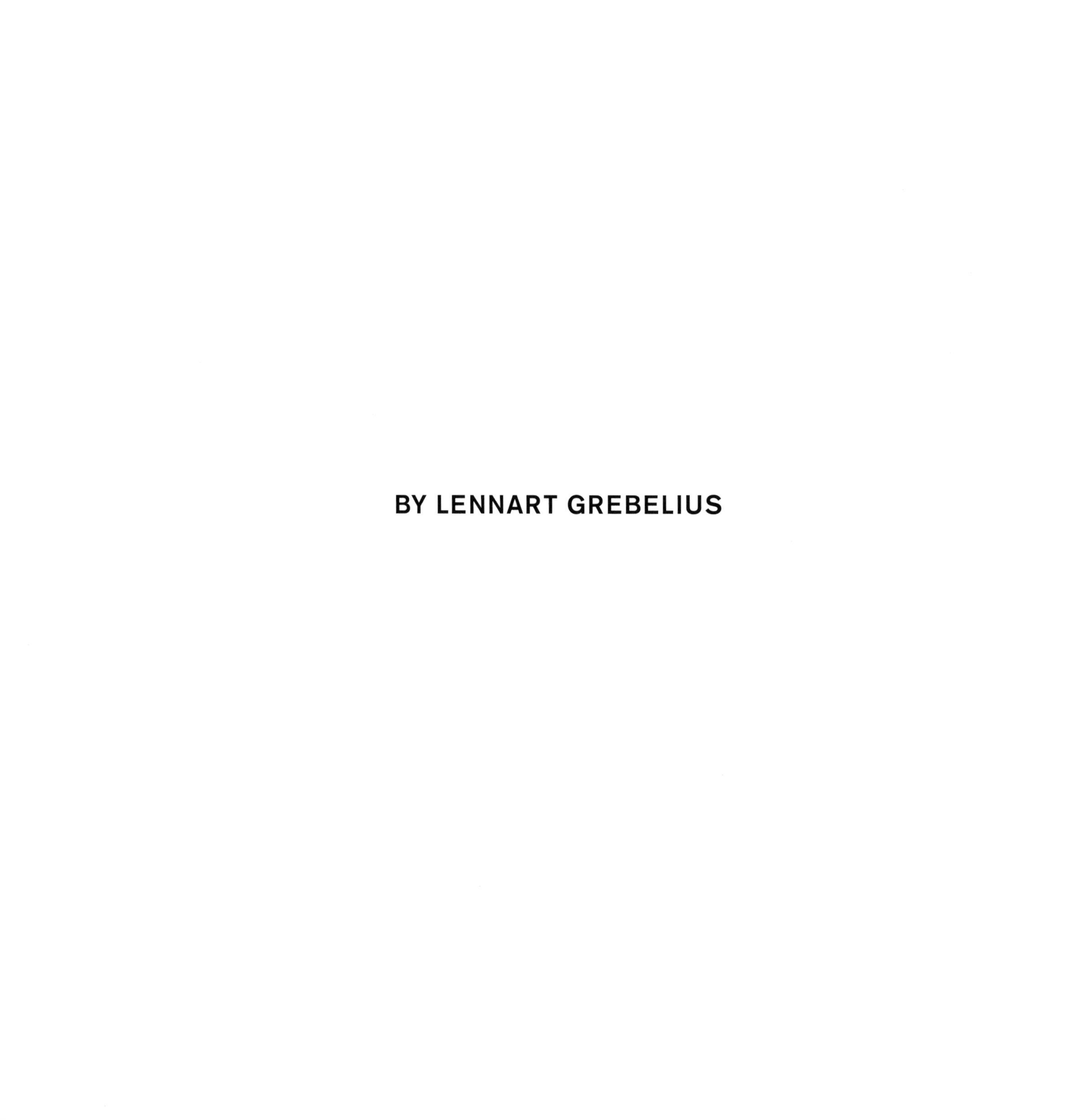

BY LENNART GREBELIUS

Of about 450 deaths that occur each year in the Texas prison system, more than 100 prisoners are unclaimed by their families and are buried at Joe Byrd Cemetery, located one mile southeast of the Huntsville Prison Unit in Huntsville, Texas.

The reason for not collecting a body of a deceased prisoner varies from case to case. Sometimes the deceased has lost contact with family and friends, sometimes the family cannot afford to arrange a funeral.

Prison funerals are generally held on Thursdays, unless the deceased has been executed, in which case the burial is often performed the following day, to save families who come to witness the execution from having to make a second trip to Huntsville. During family visits, death row inmates and their relatives are separated by a glass wall preventing any physical contact.

An arrangement can be discussed with the warden and a local church so that immediately after an execution, prison staff will place the body on a gurney and let the family visit it at the church. It may be the first time in years that family members are able to touch their relative. The body is still warm and it becomes a meaningful time for the families, before the body turns cold and stiff.

Sometimes family and friends of the deceased attend the funeral and sometimes no one comes. Either way, the chaplain of the Walls Unit leads the graveside services. If no family attends, the services are held in the presence of the Walls Unit warden or designee as well as the officer and the inmates whose job it is to care for the cemetery. It is not unusual to have multiple burials in a single day. At times, there are up to four funerals in a morning. Inmates are buried in a simple casket, which is placed inside a two-piece hard plastic shell.

Rows of grave markers made of rebar-reinforced concrete cover the gently sloping hill of the graveyard. Prisoners make the markers on-site in a small shed. Some headstones include the inmate's name and the dates of birth and death, however, others include only prisoner numbers and dates of death. A prisoner number beginning with "999" indicates that the inmate was put on death row. If the inmate was executed the stones bear the letter "X."

This cemetery is the largest prison cemetery in the State of Texas. The first prisoners were interred there in the mid-1800s. From early on, the cemetery was known as Peckerwood Hill. Southern blacks used "Peckerwood" as a derogatory term to describe poor and/or rural southern whites.

Huntsville is the headquarters of the Texas state prison system and has the busiest lethal injection team in America. About 8,500 inmates—who are counted in the city's population of 35,500—call Huntsville home. Thousands of local residents work for the Department of Criminal Justice, which is the city's largest employer.

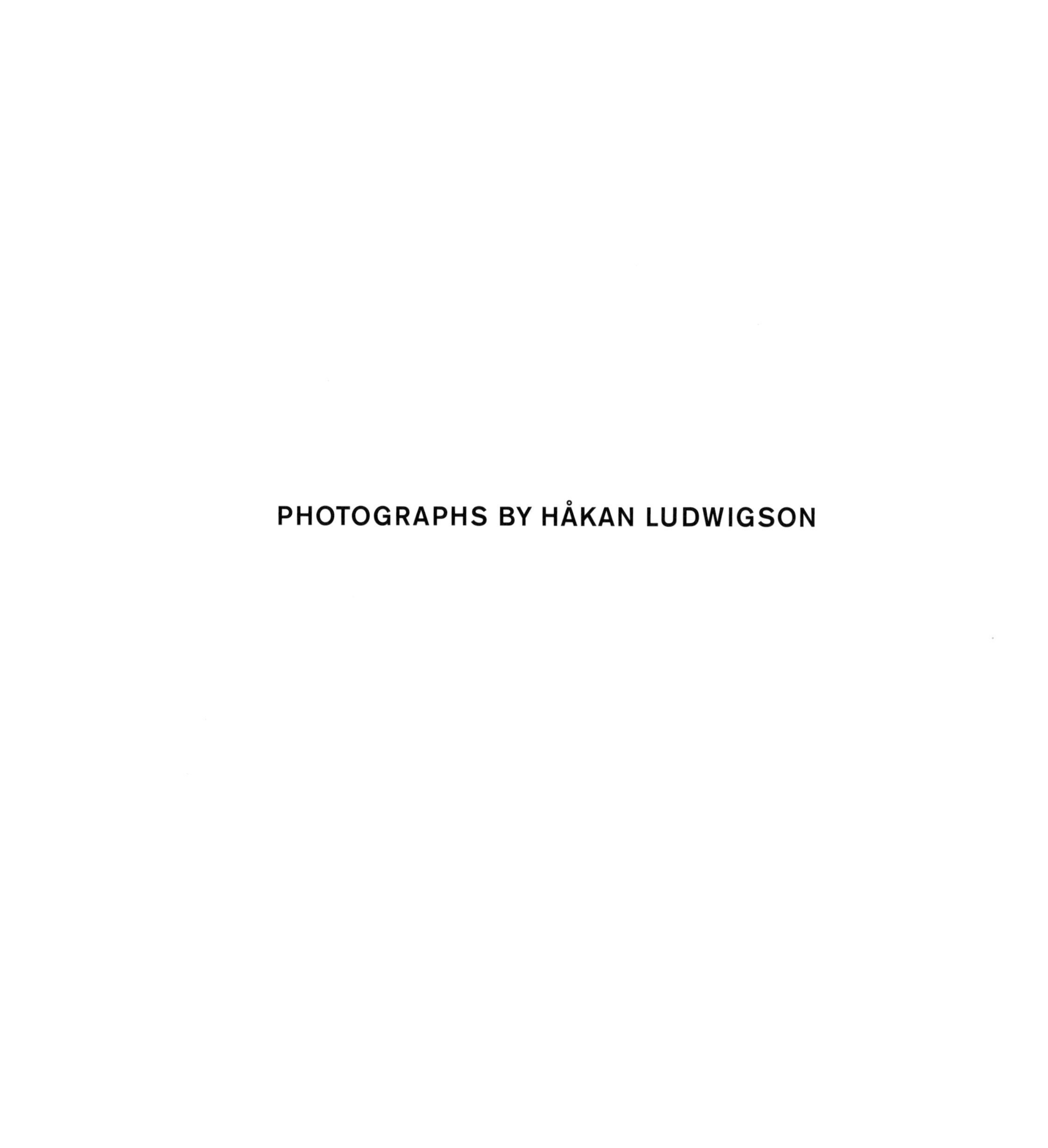

PHOTOGRAPHS BY HÅKAN LUDWIGSON

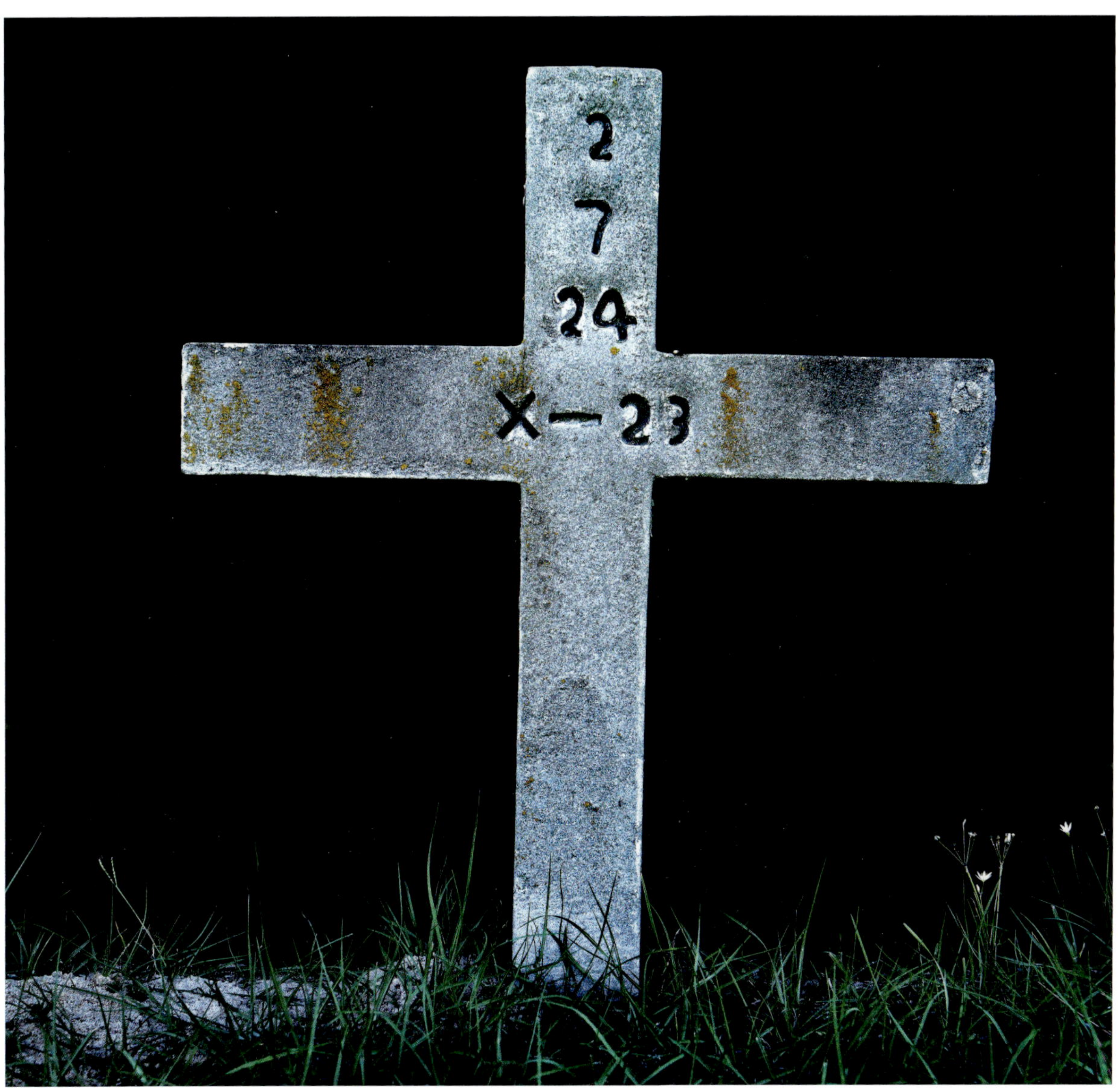

#056

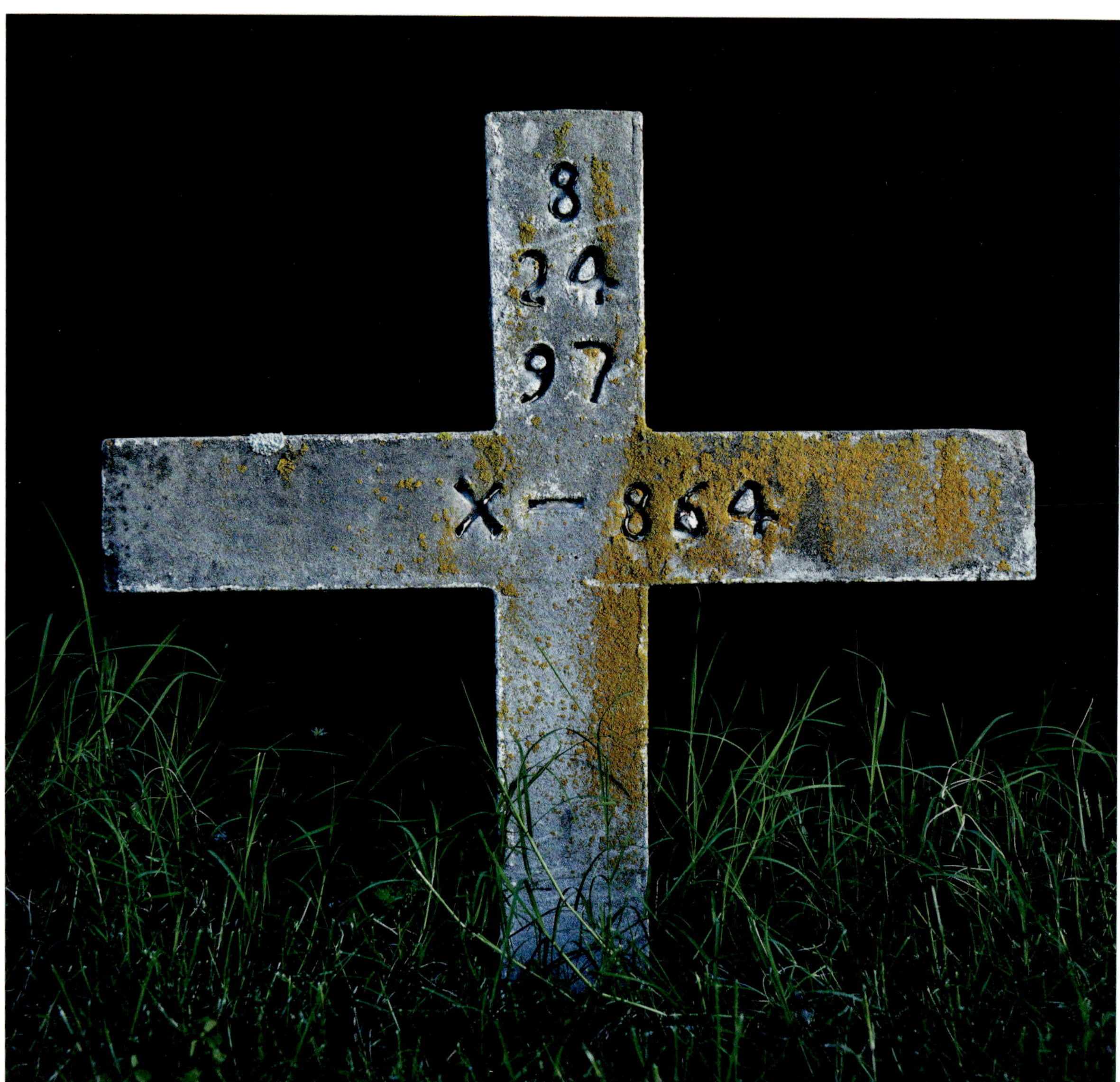

#123

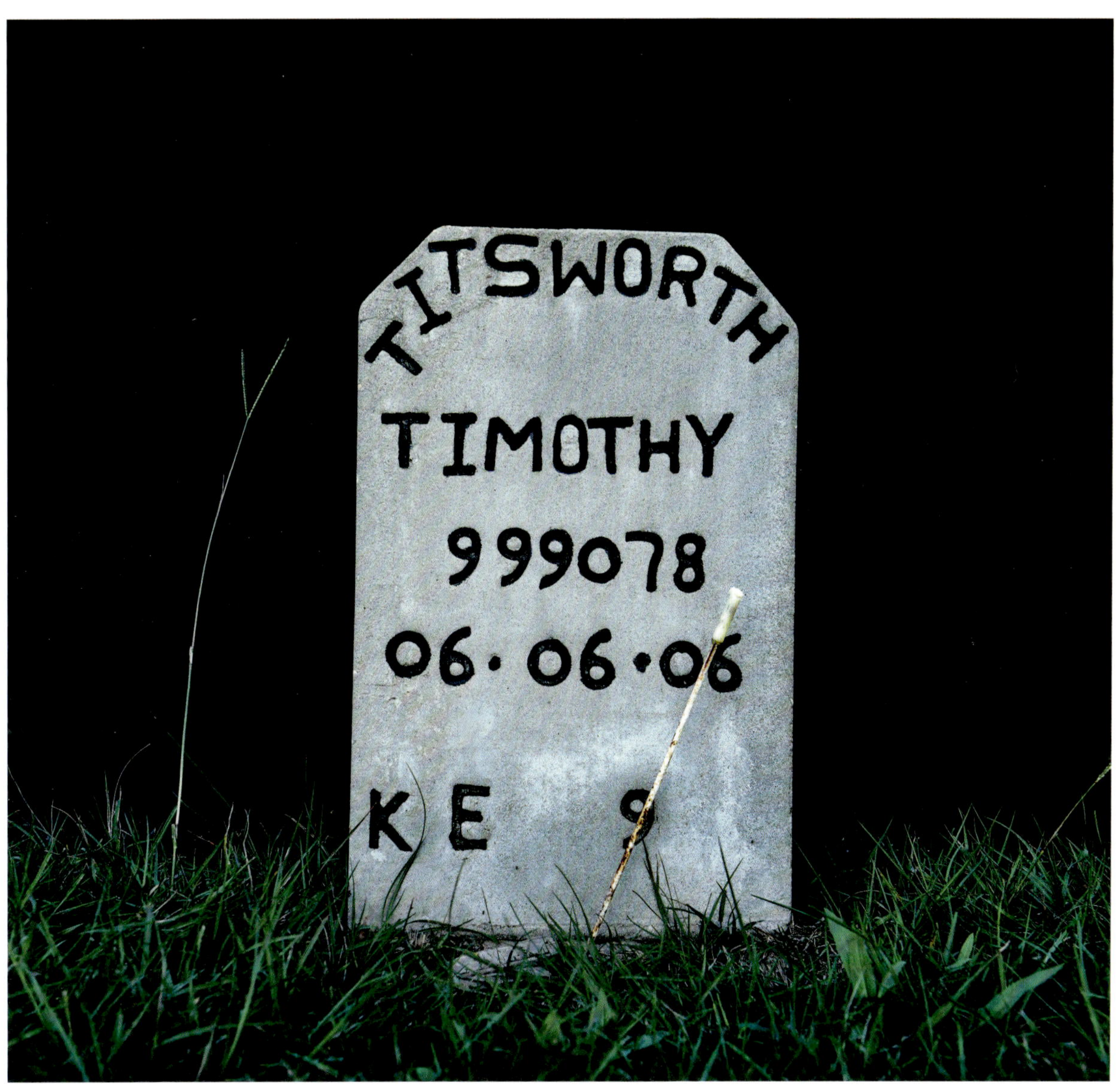

#092

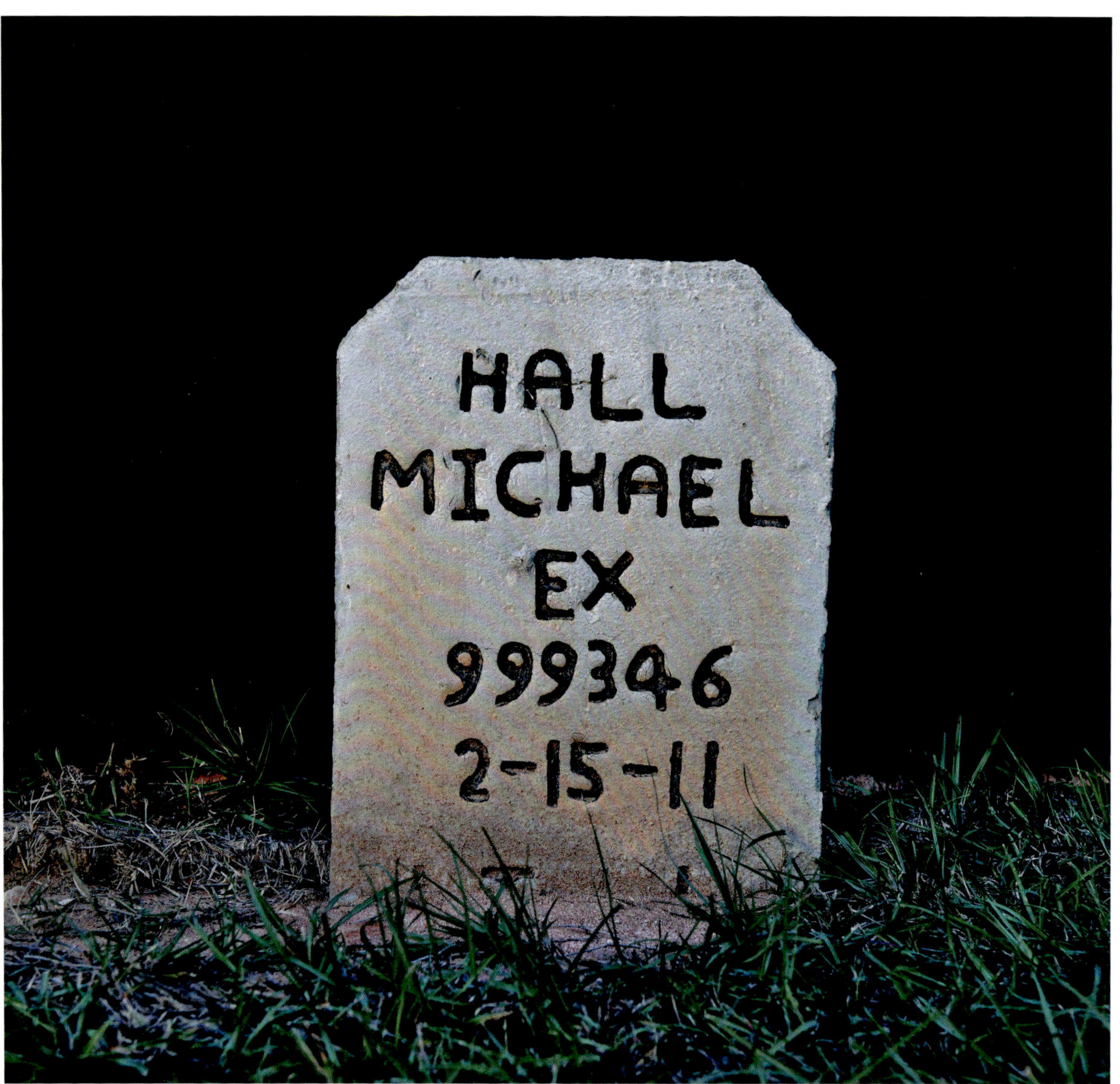

#094

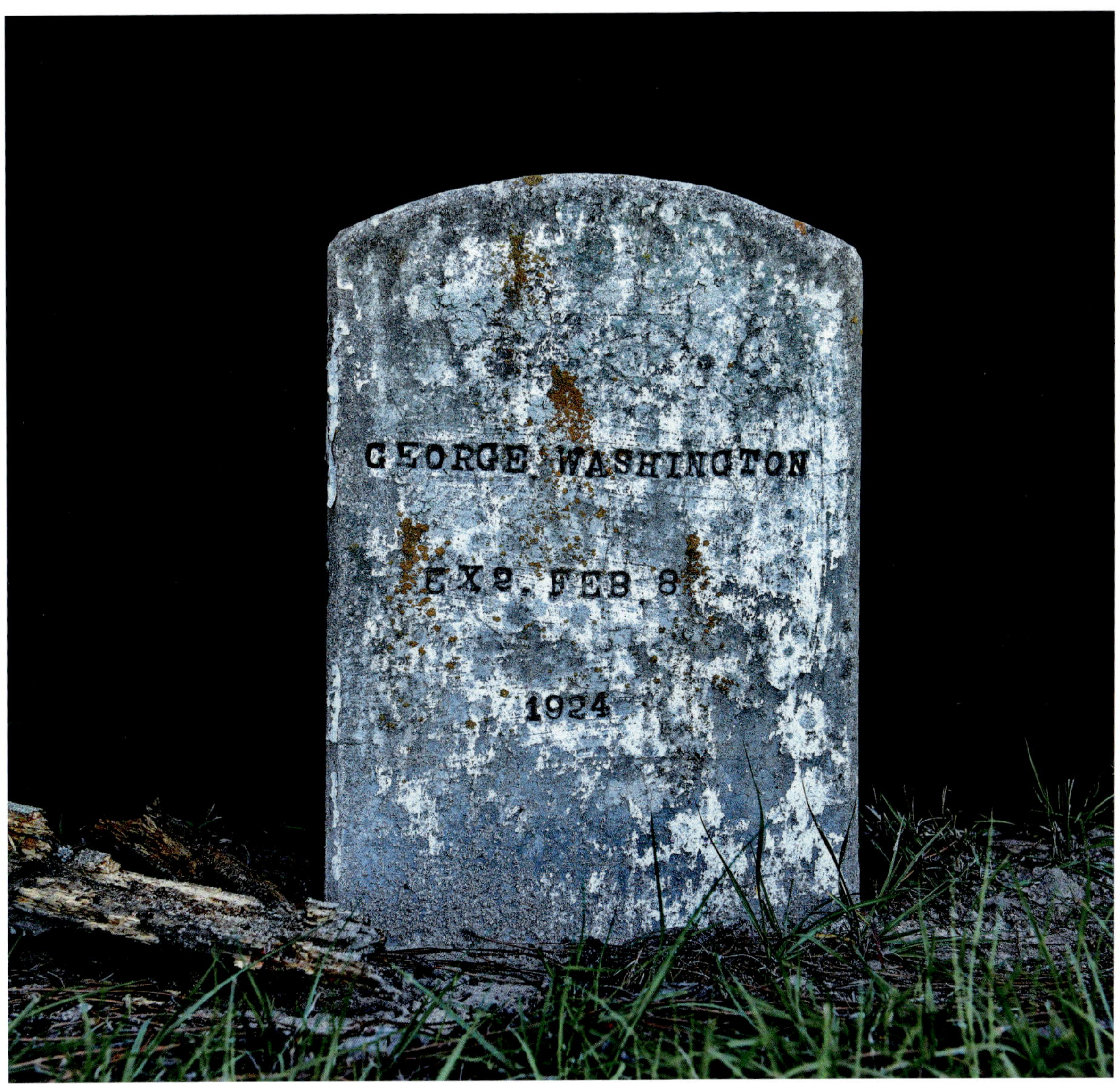

#049

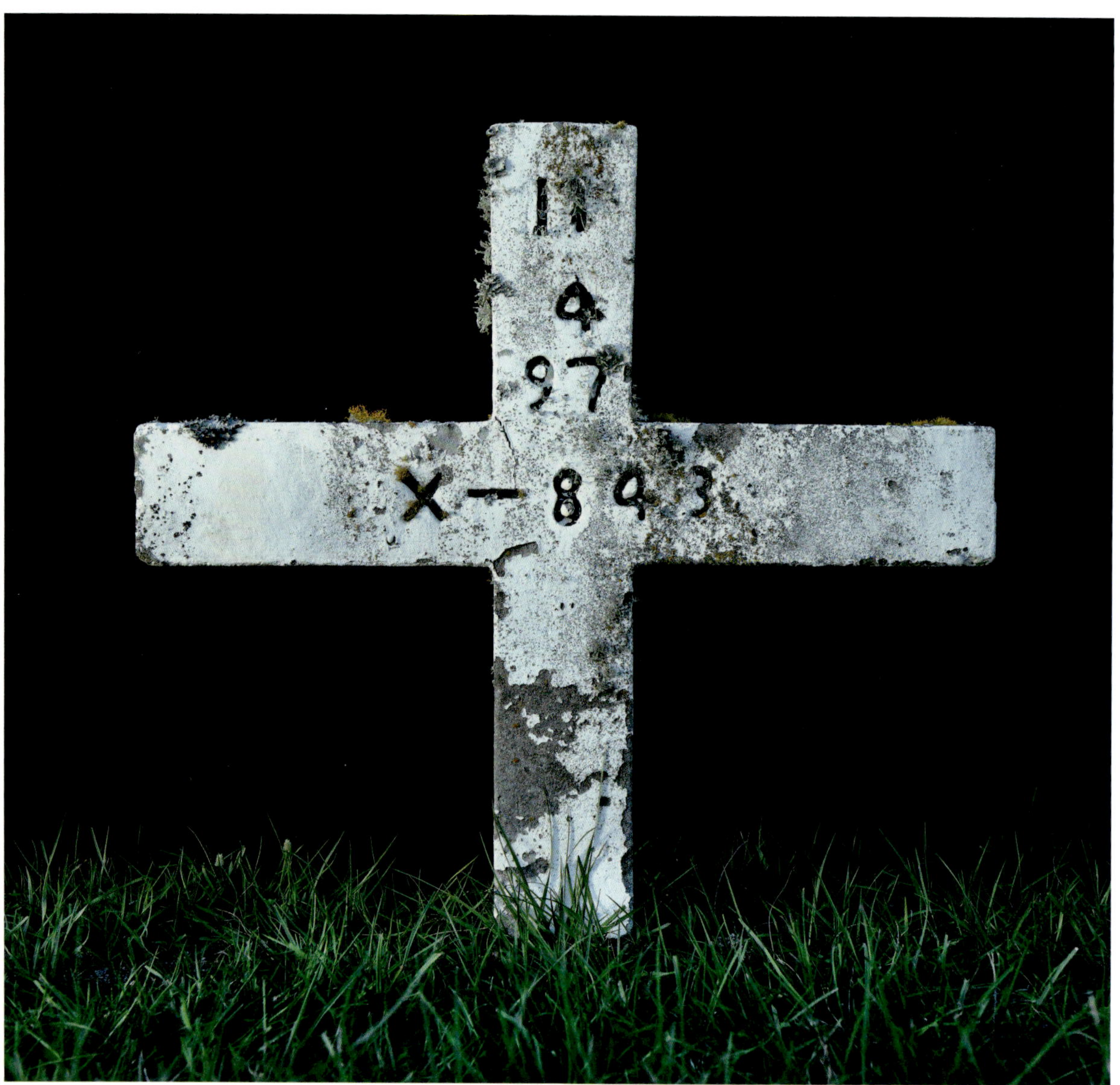

#116

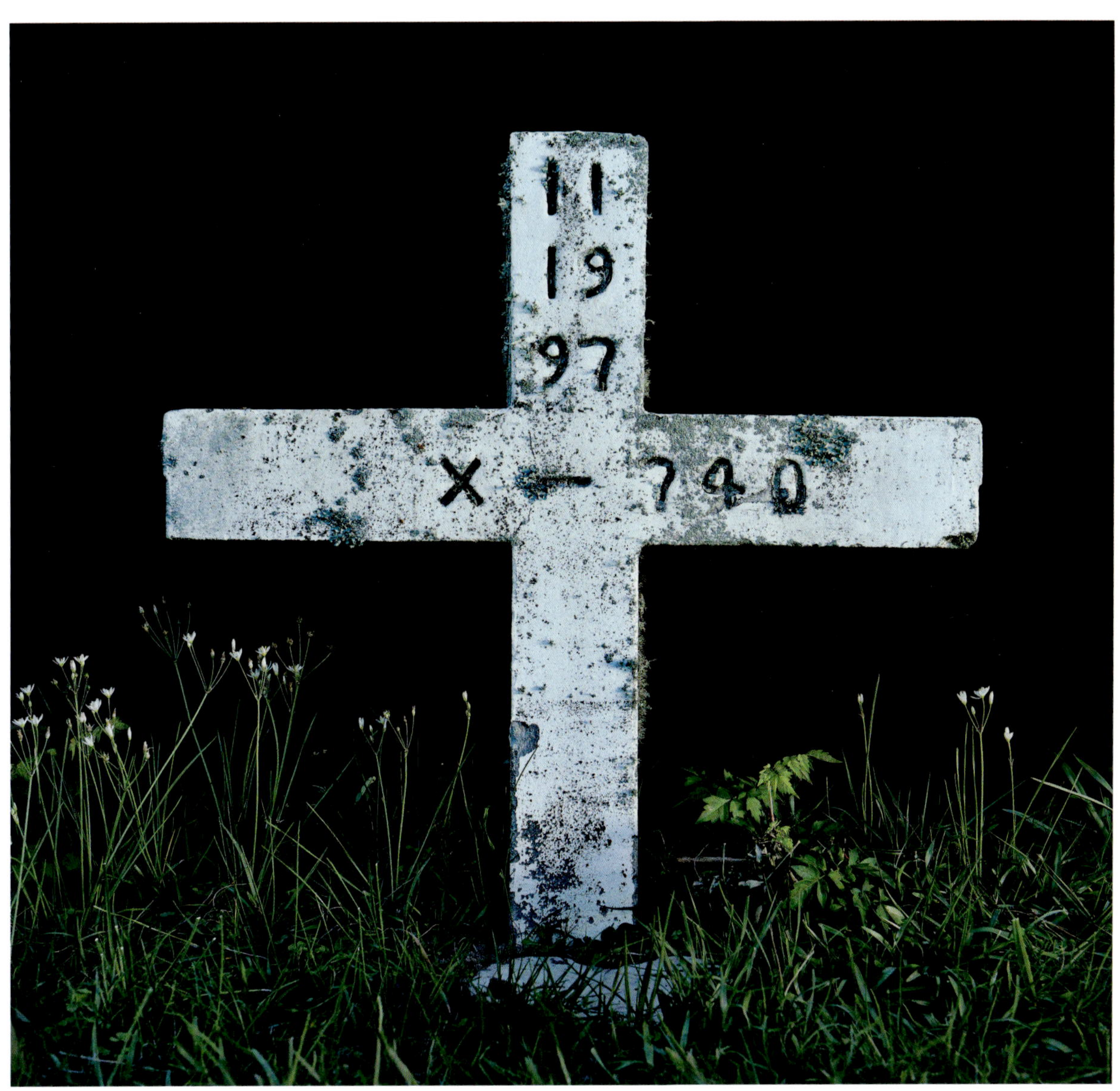

#117

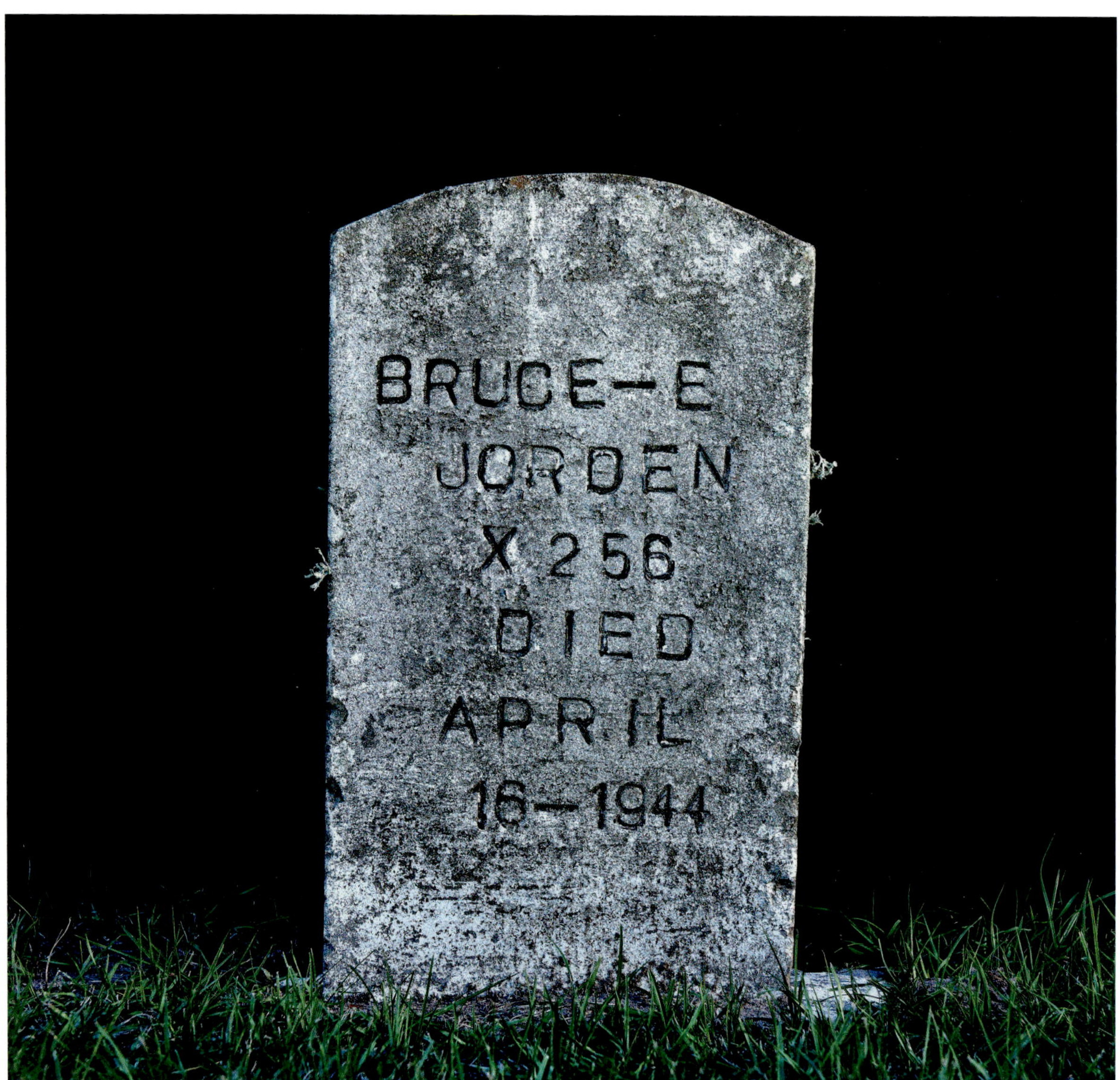

#113

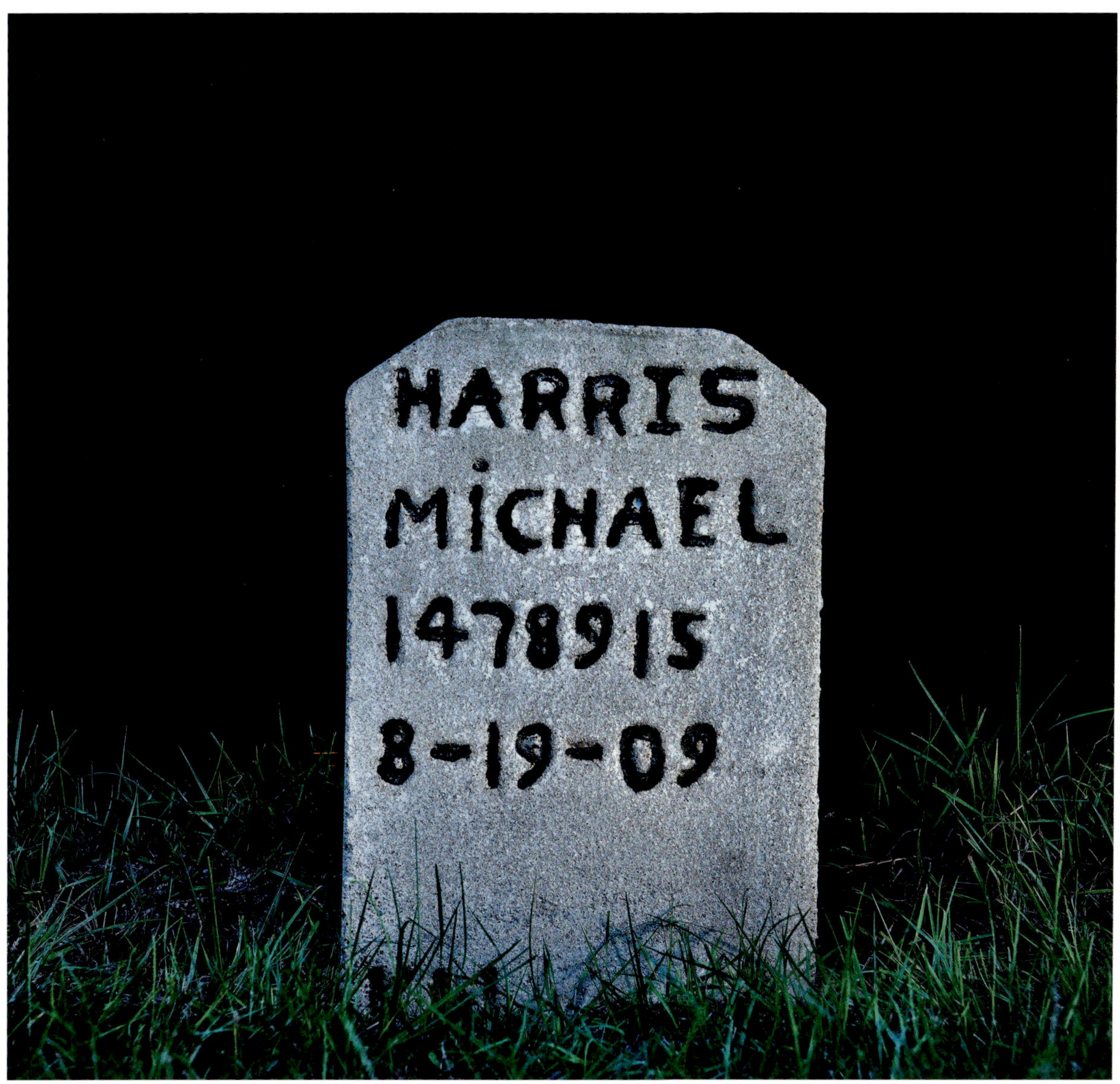

#101

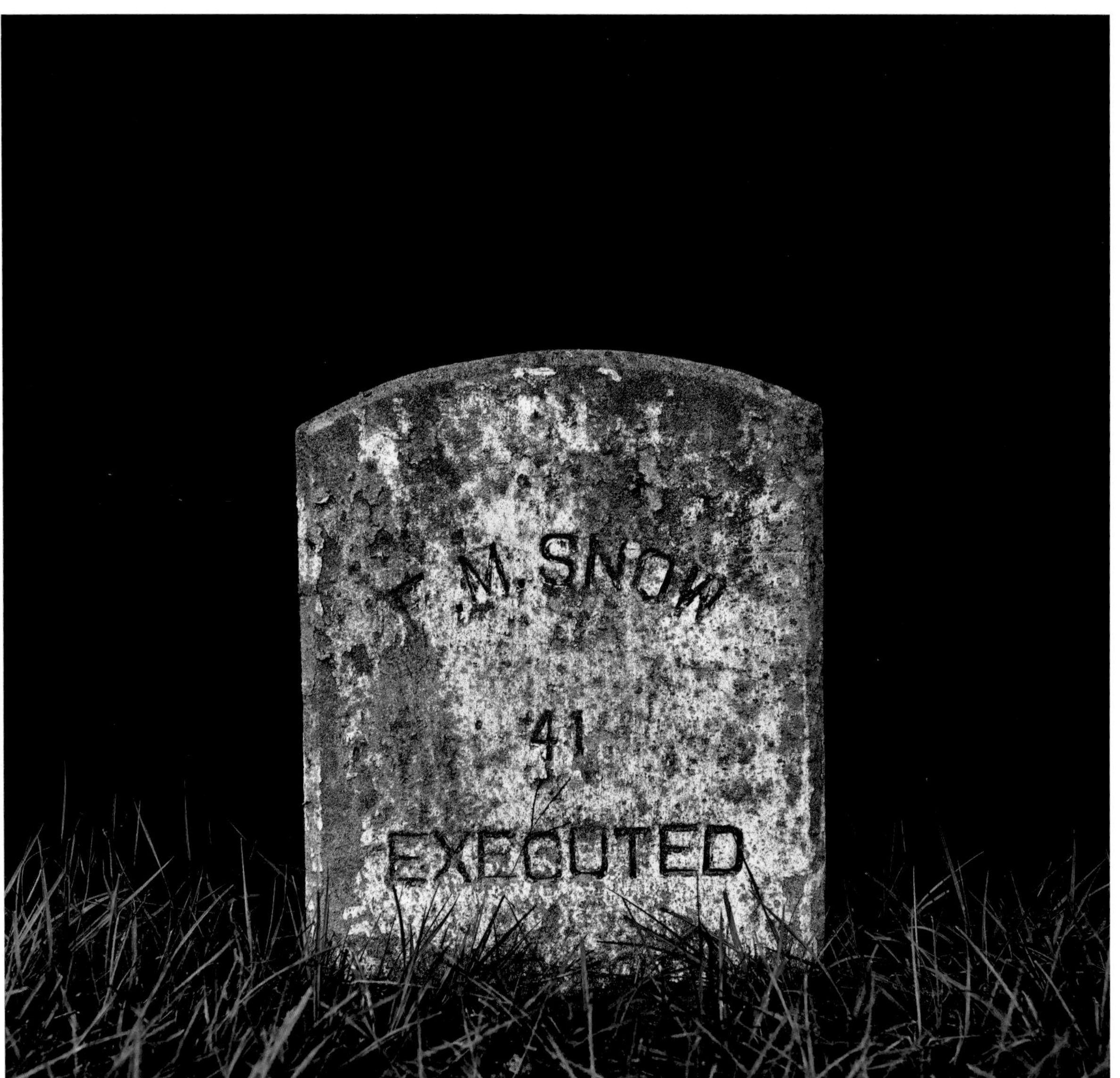

#005

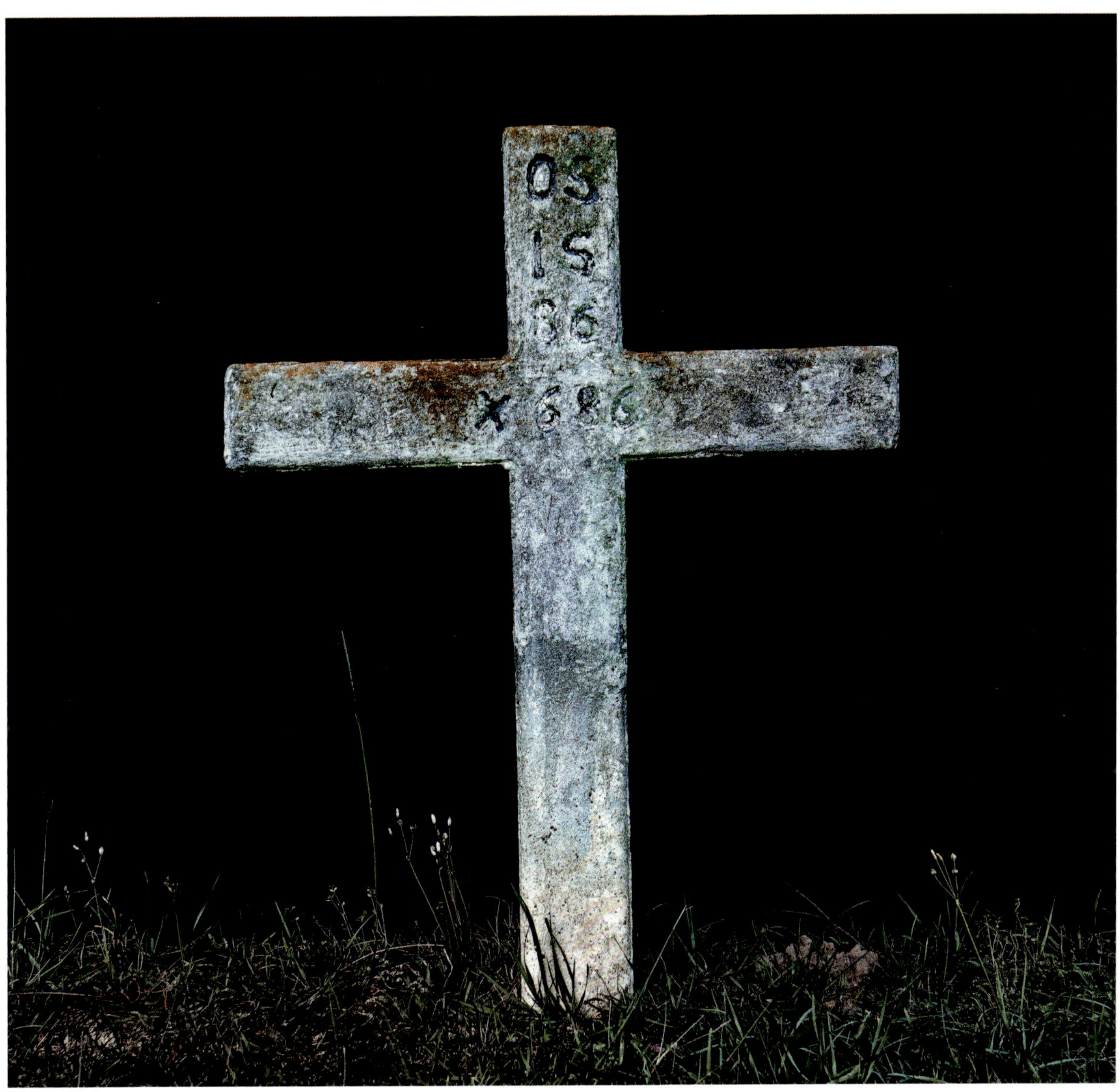

#030

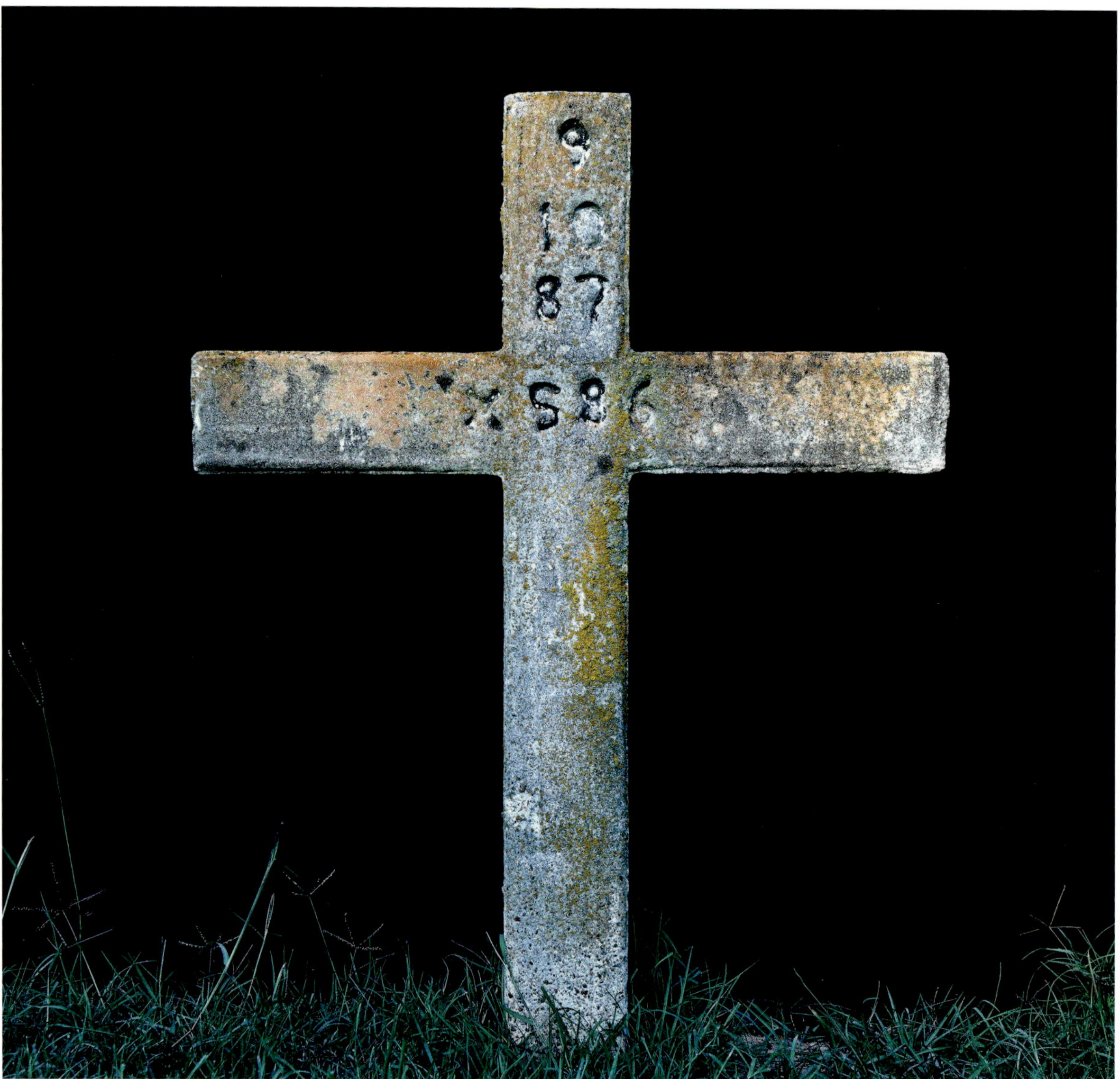

#031

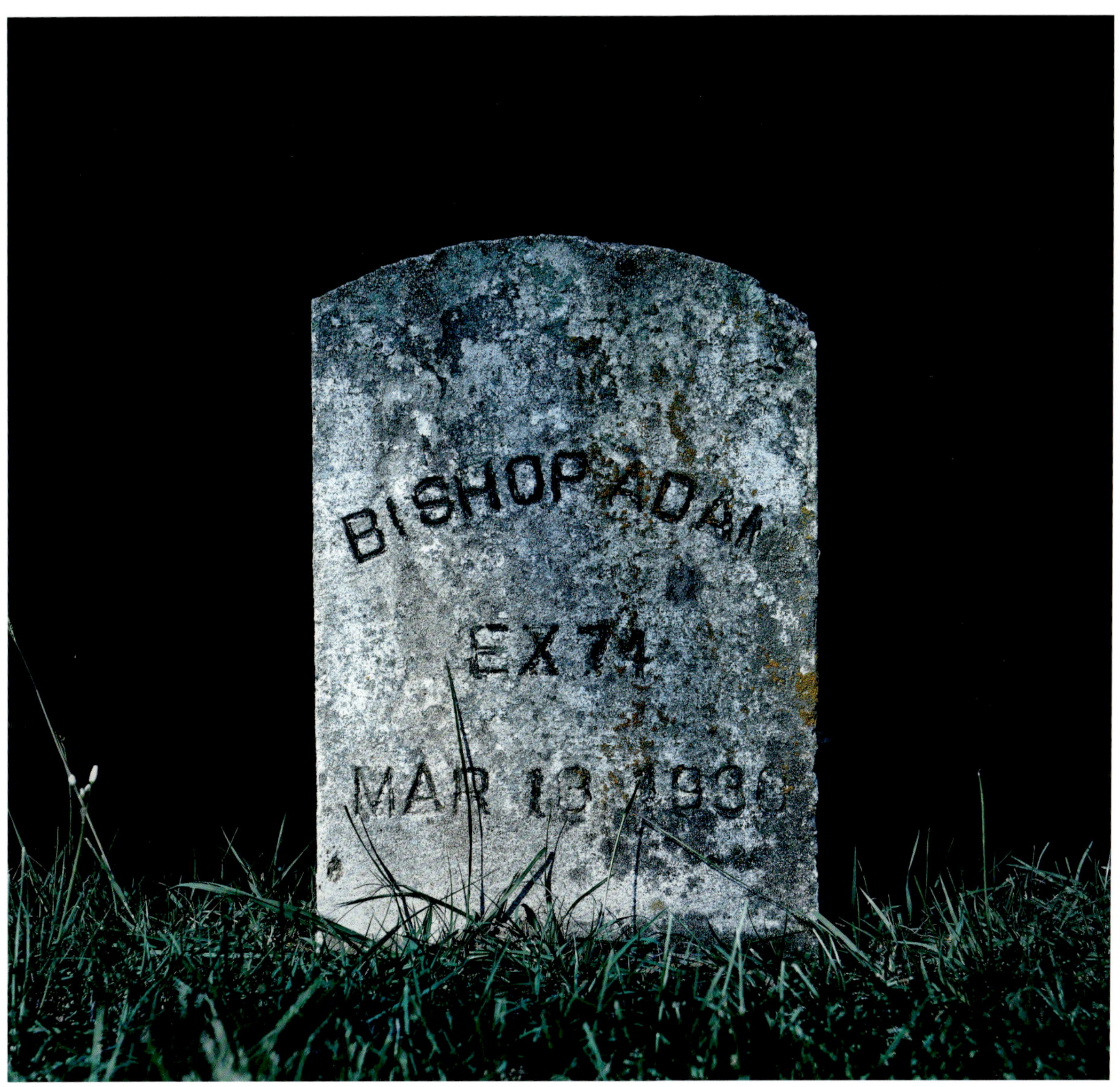

#040

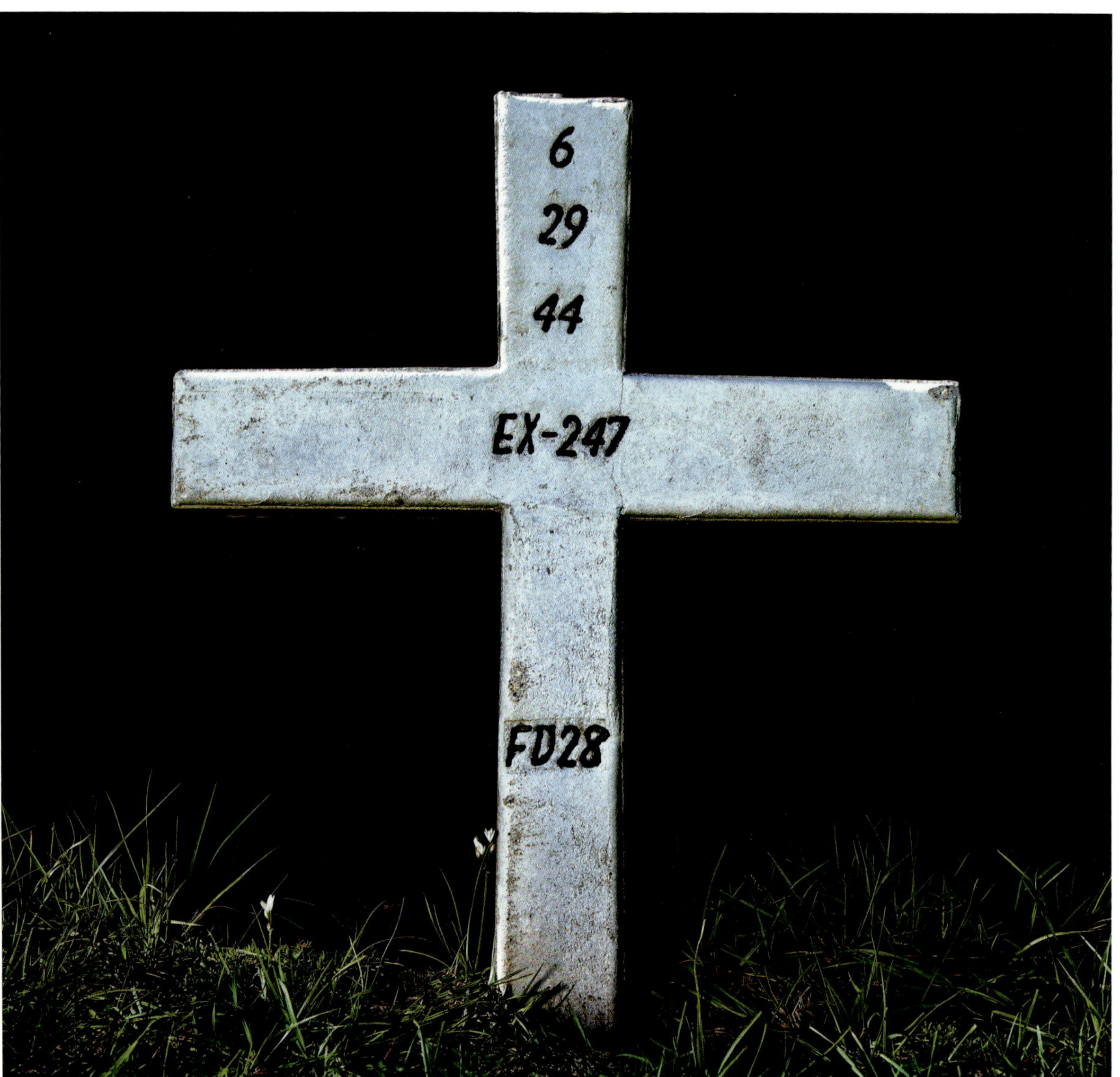

6
29
44
EX-247
FD28

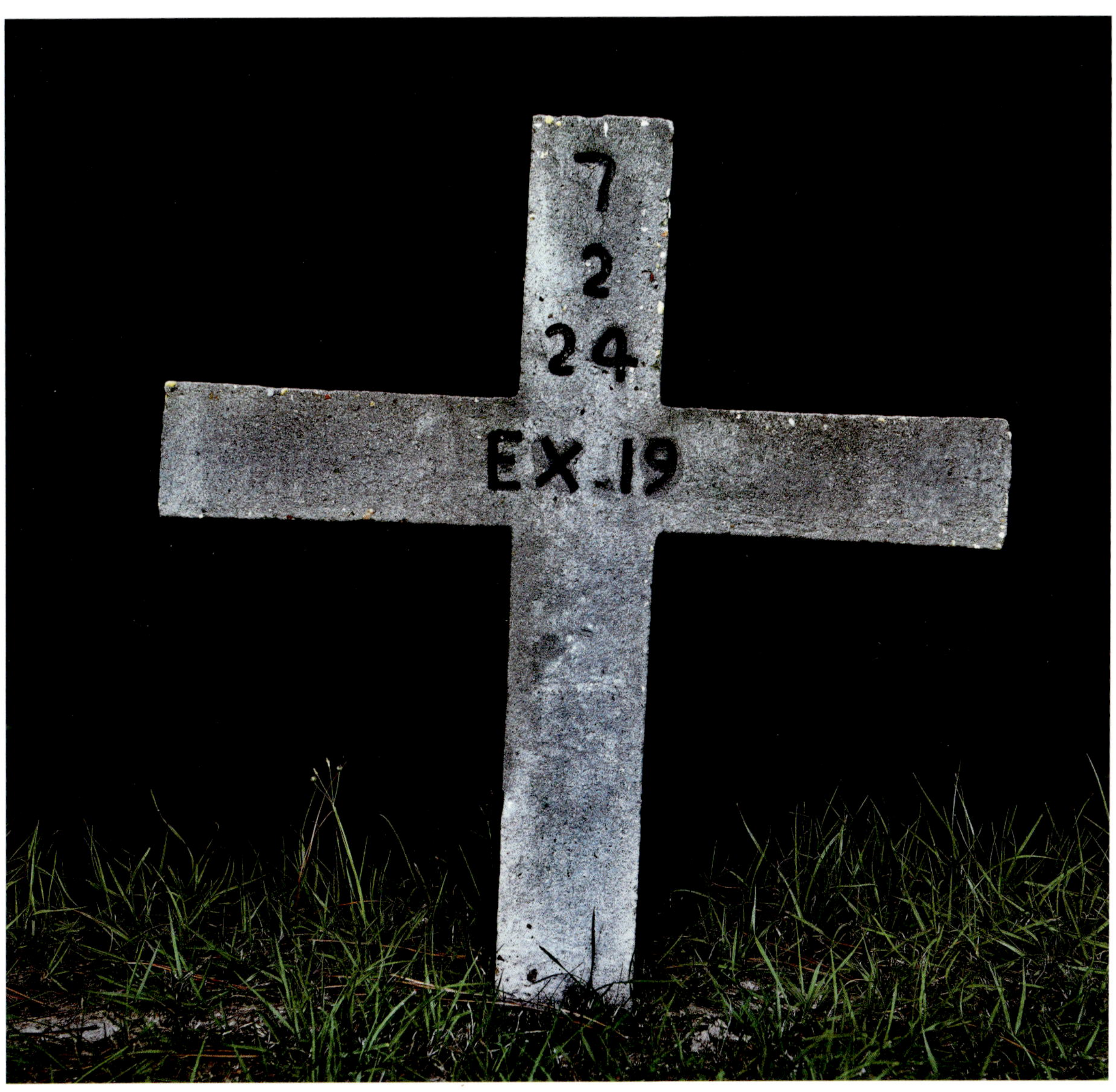

#054

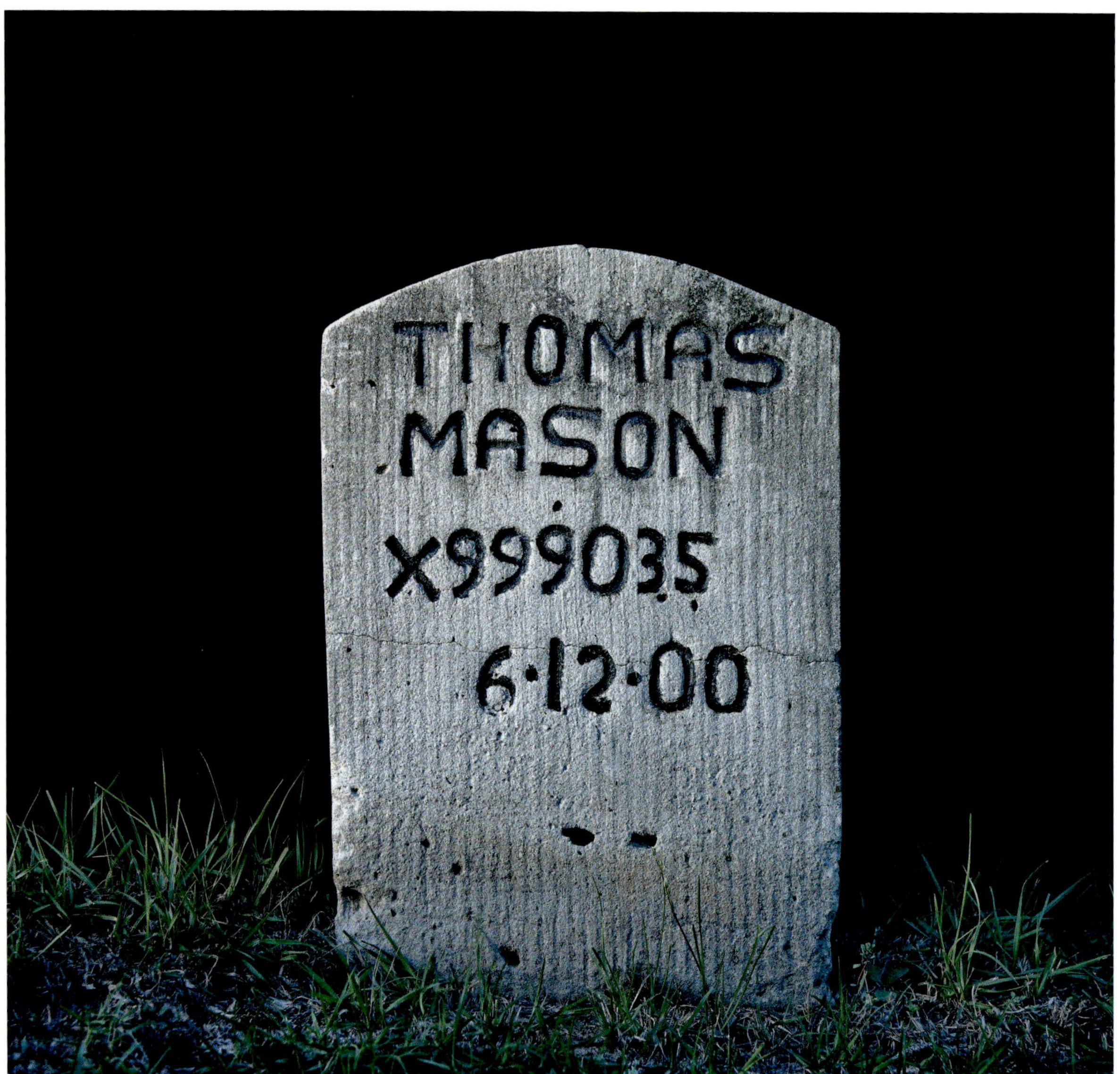

#062

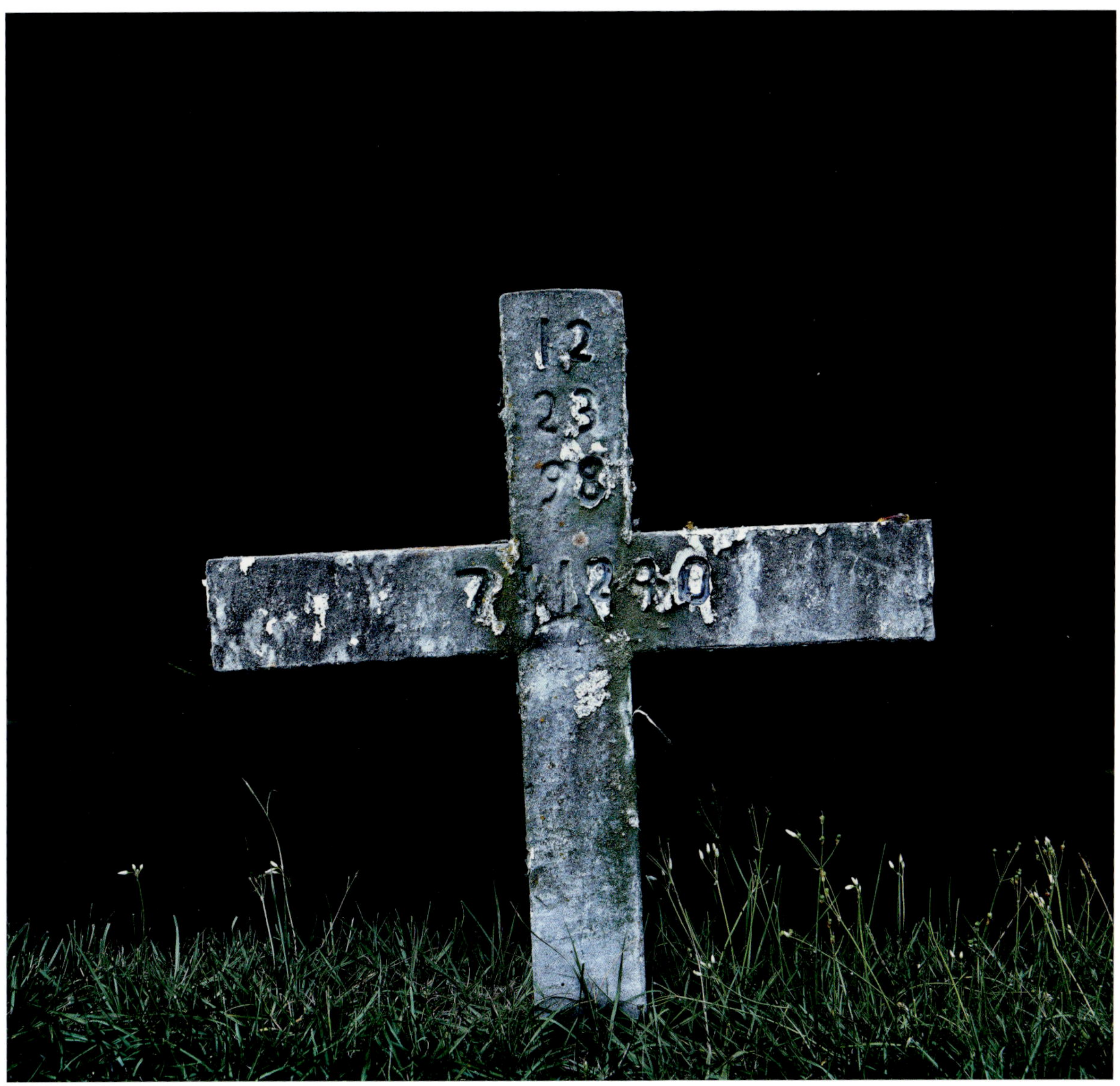

#164

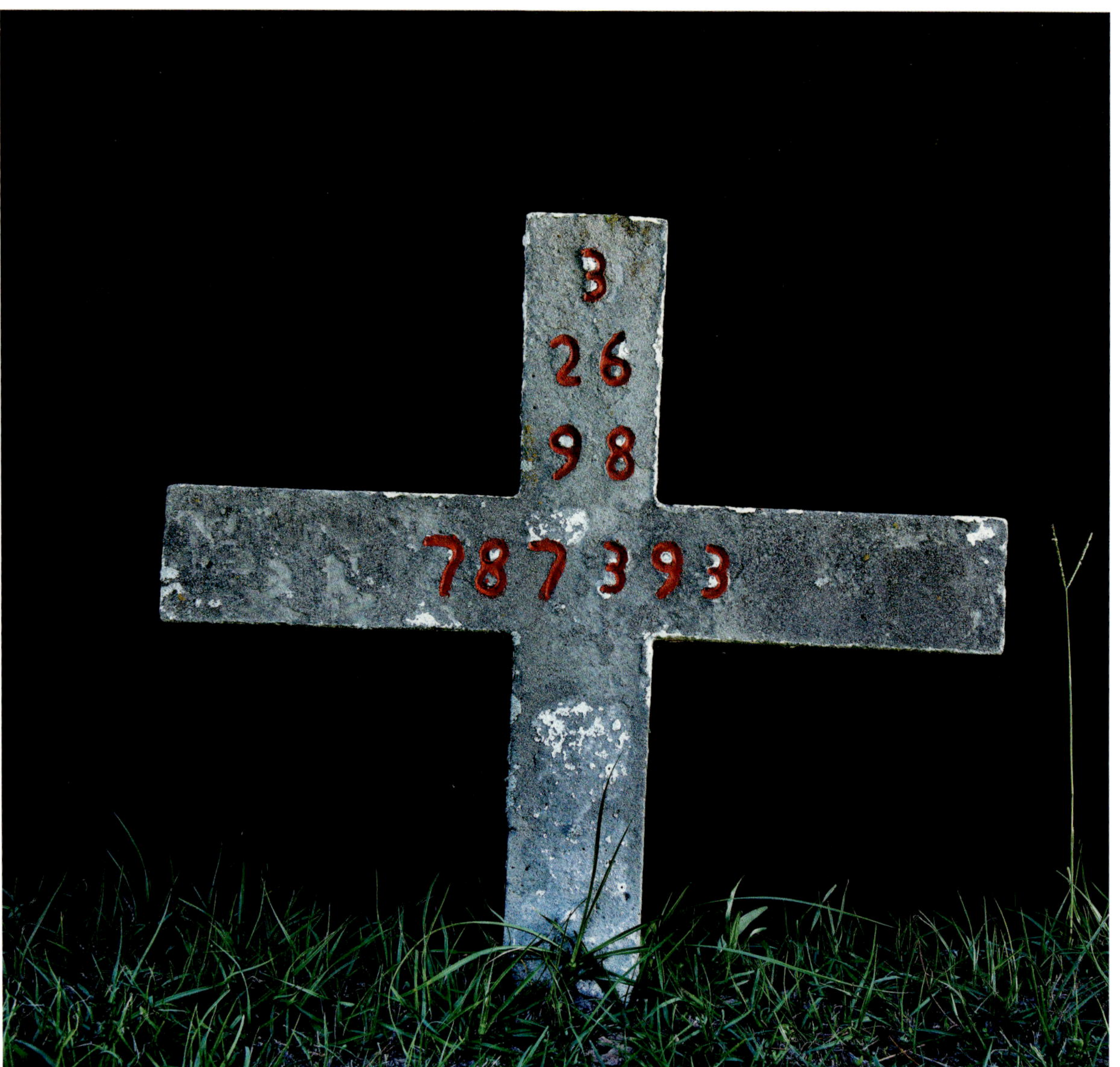

#154

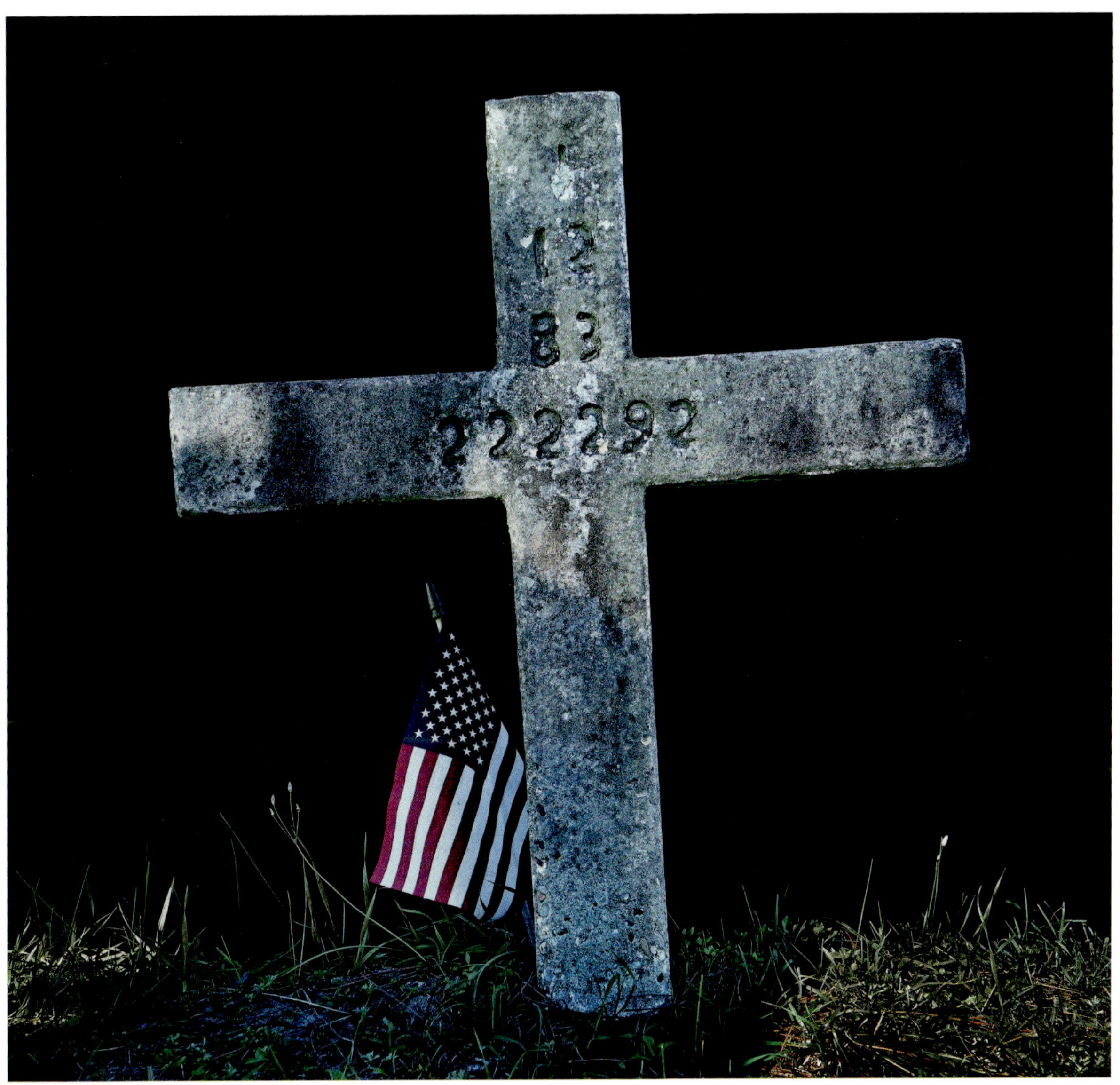

#039

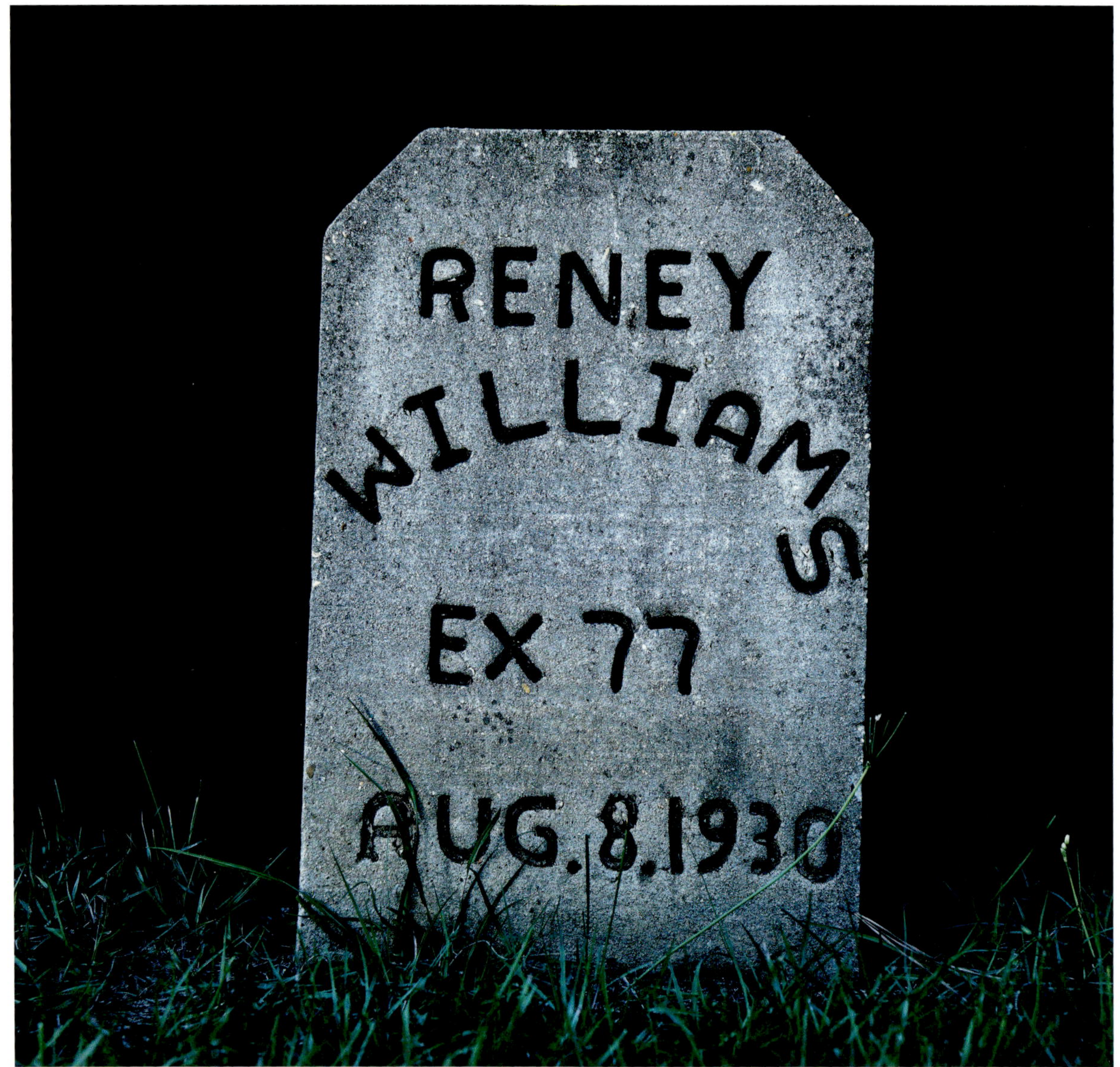

#044

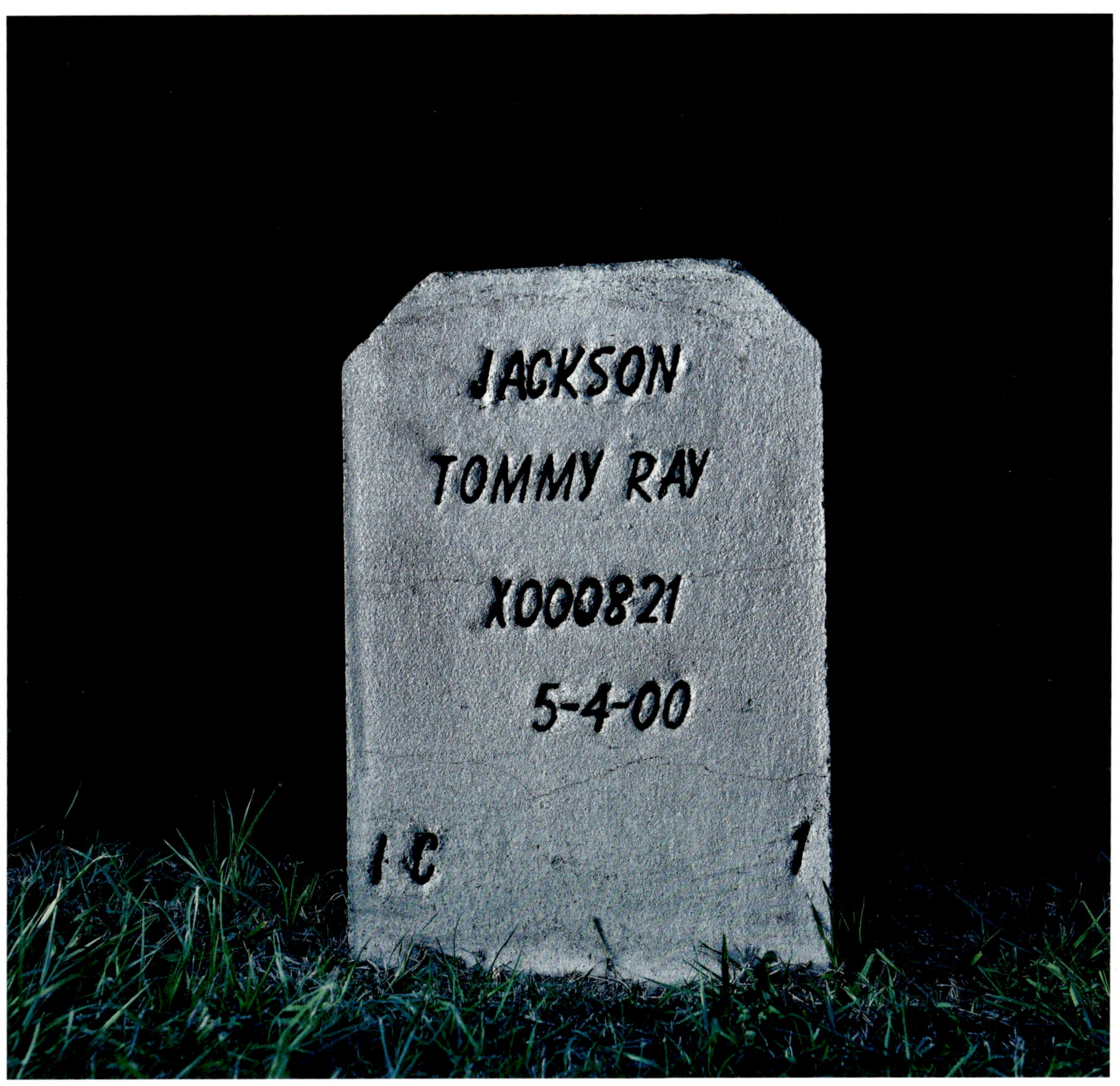

#061

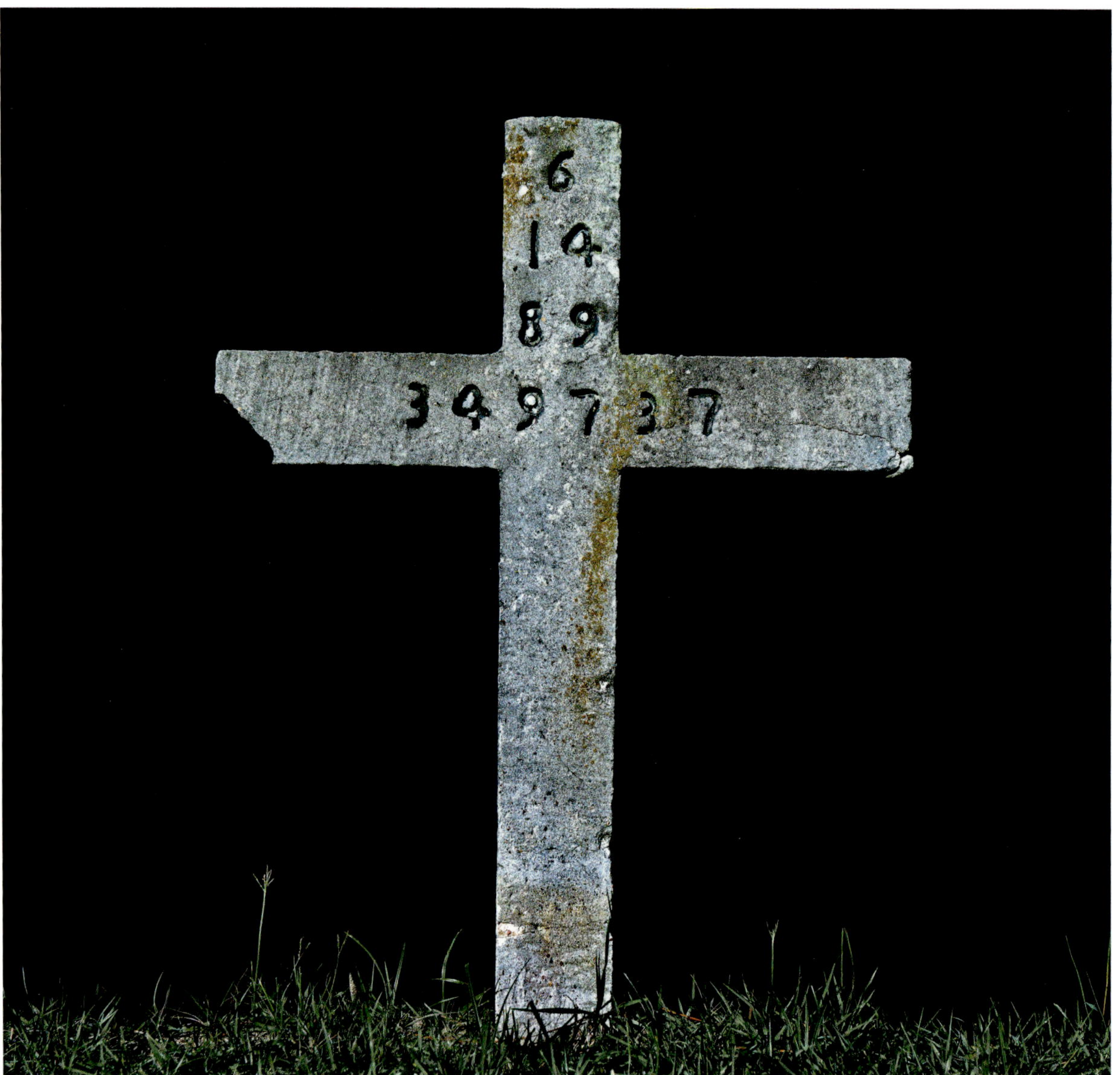
6
14
89
3 4 9 7 3 7

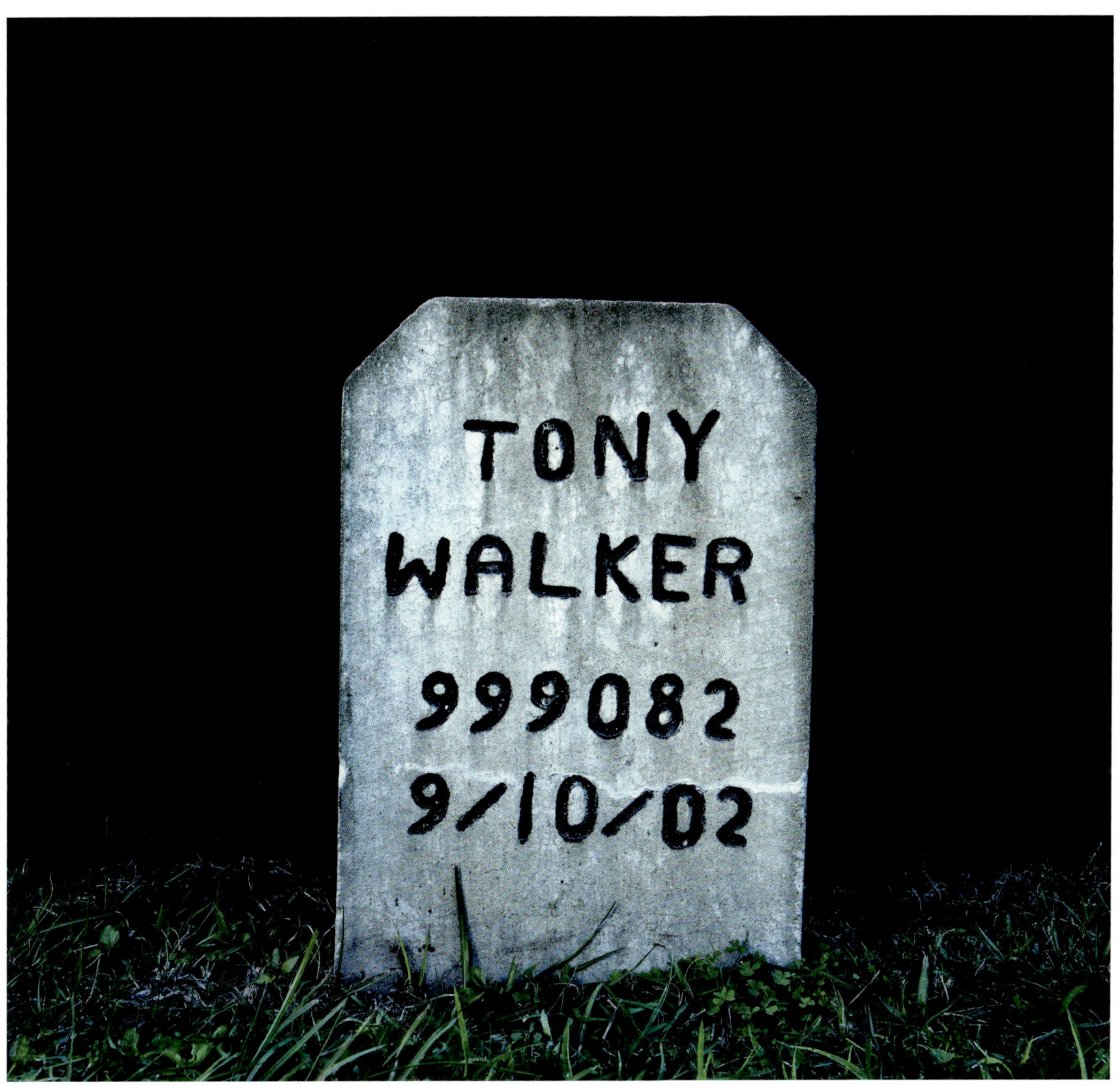

#070

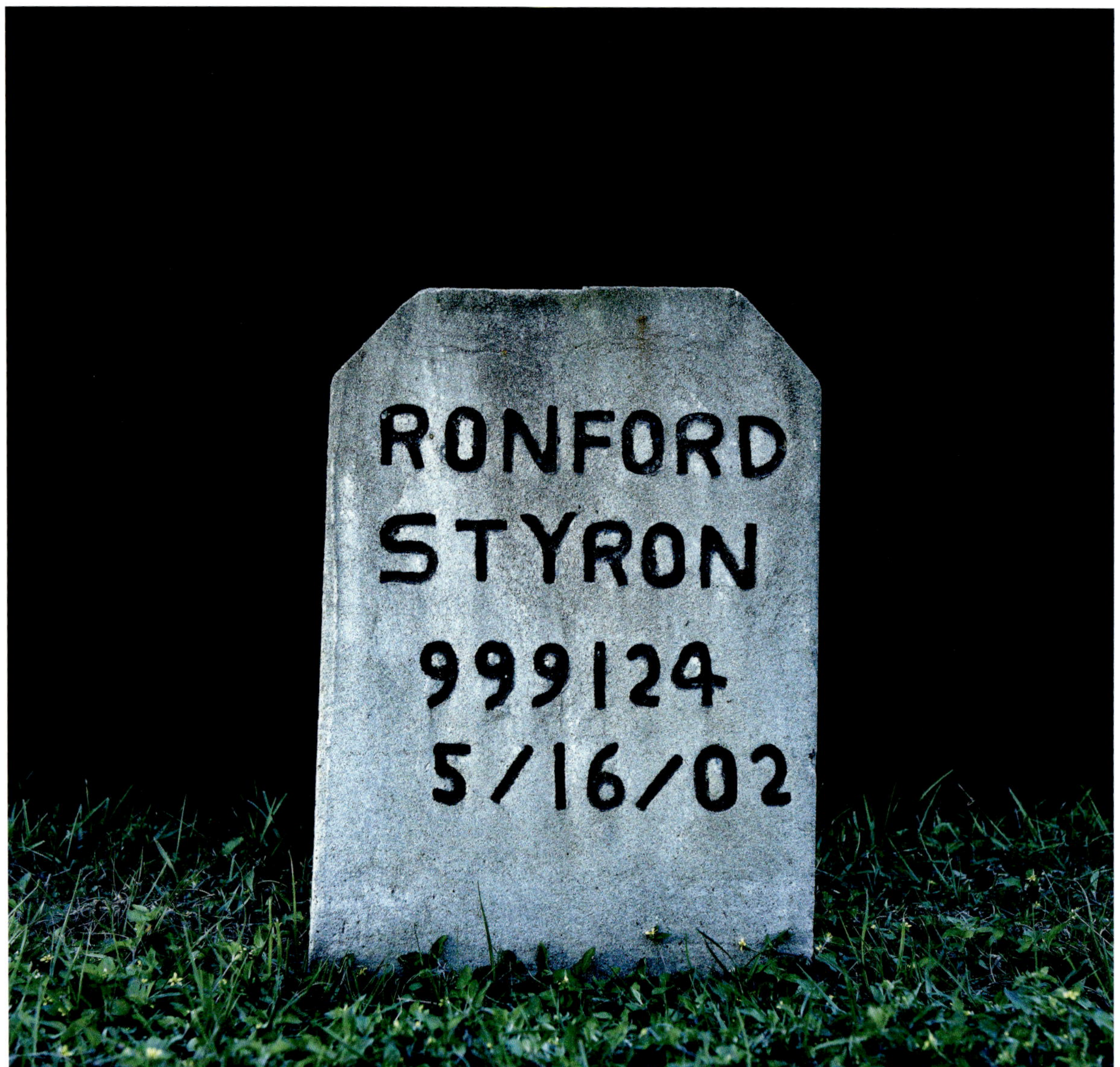
RONFORD
STYRON
999124
5/16/02

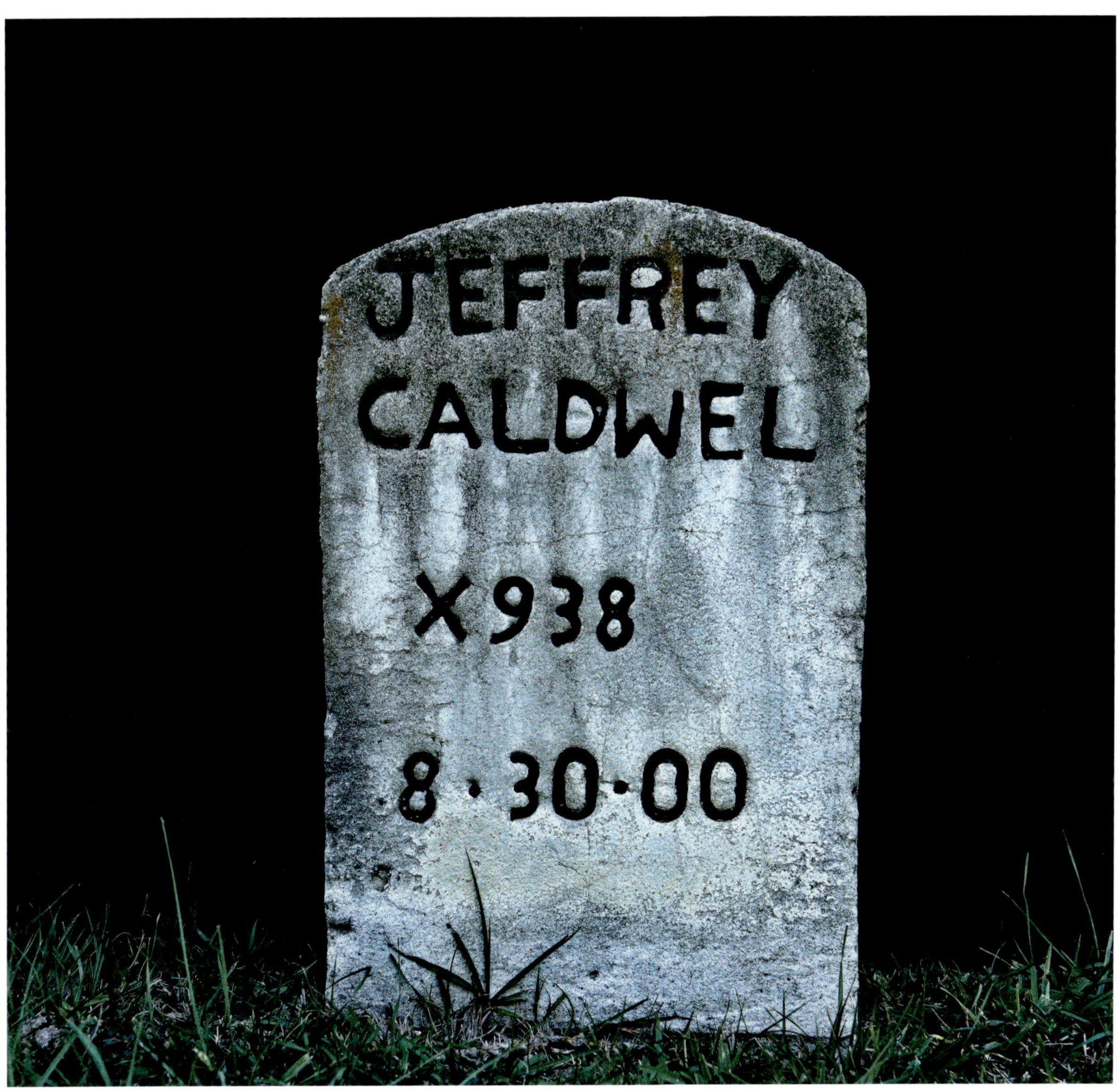

#063

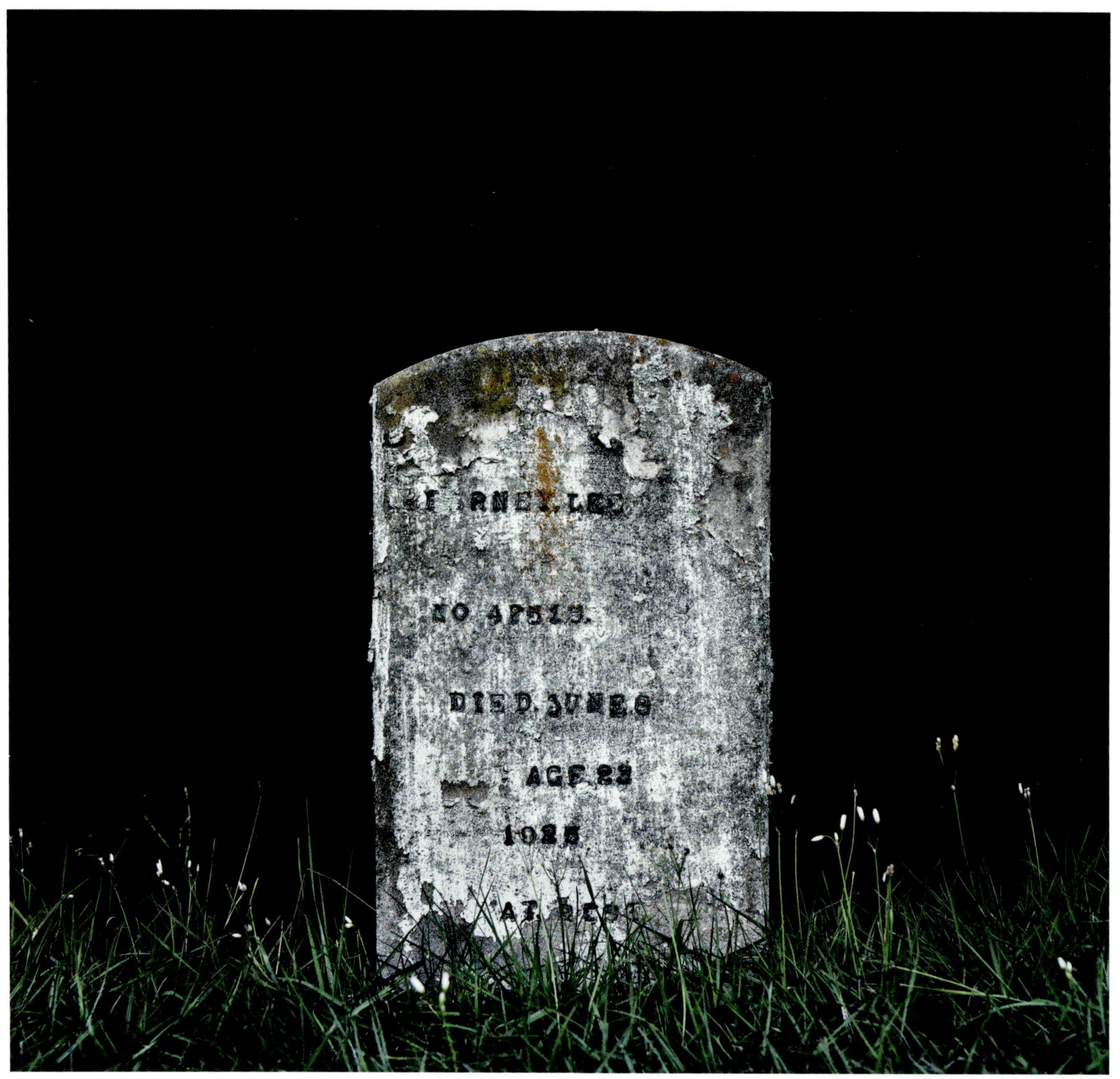

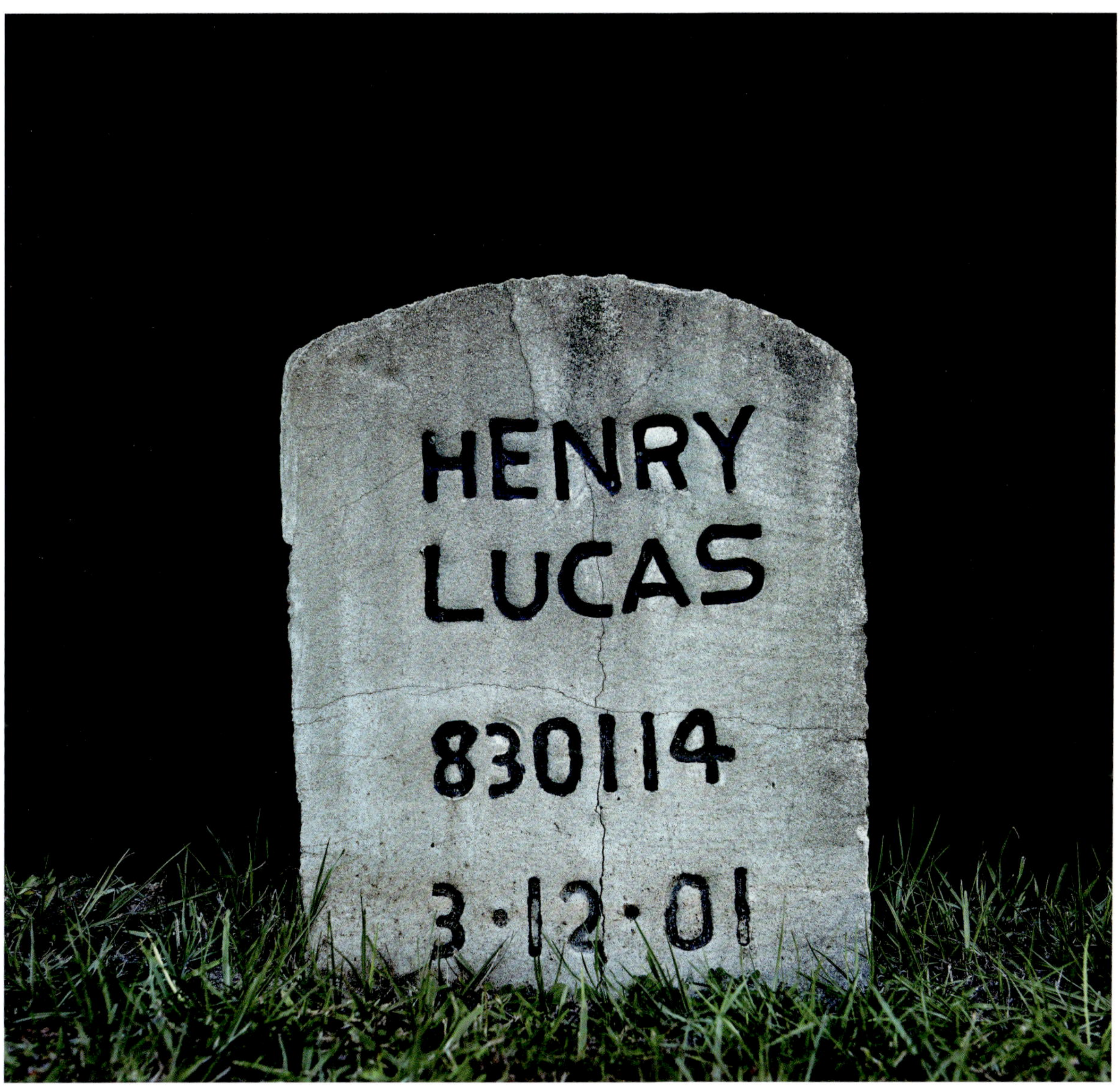

#066

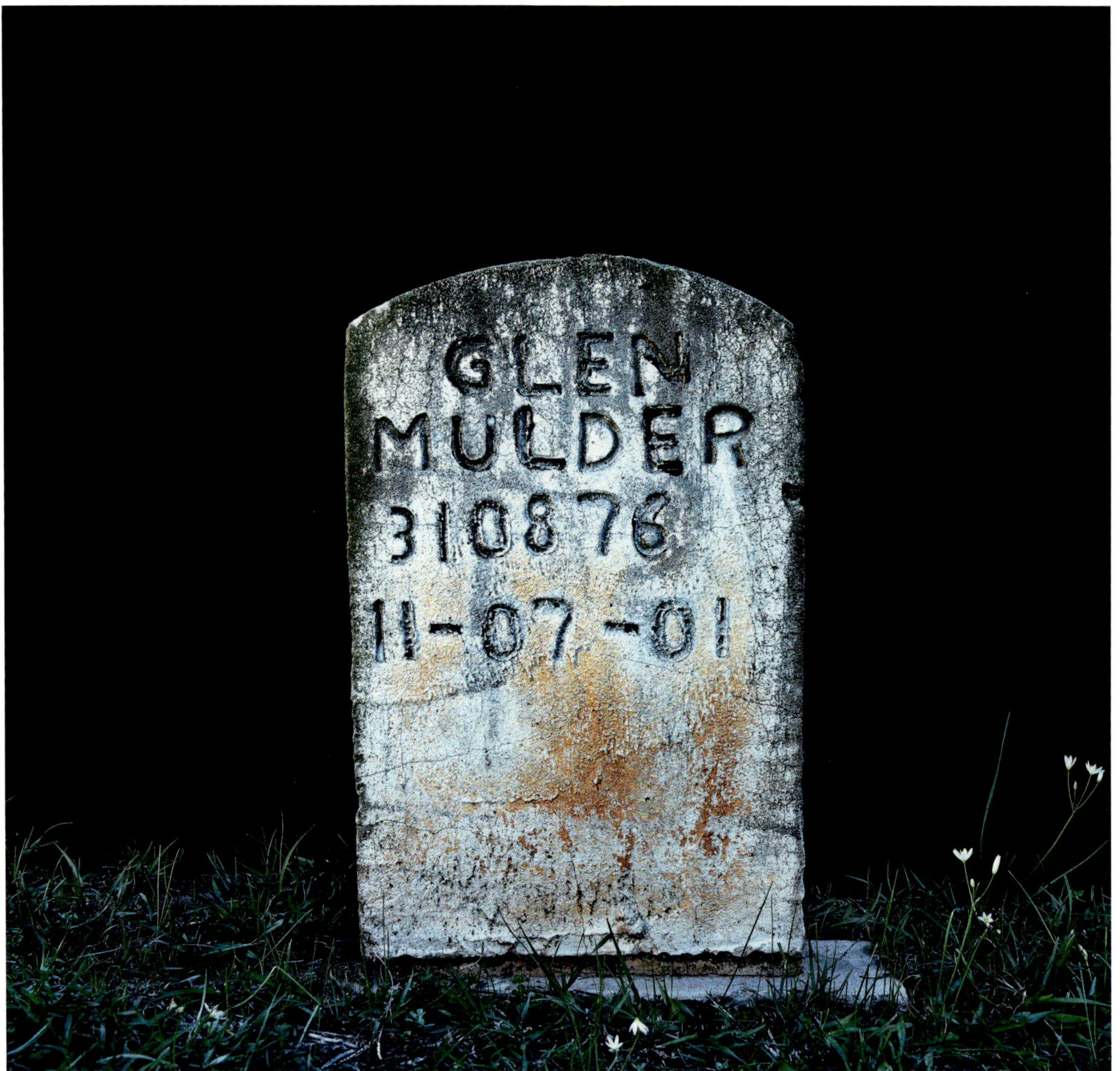

GLEN
MULDER
310876
11-07-01

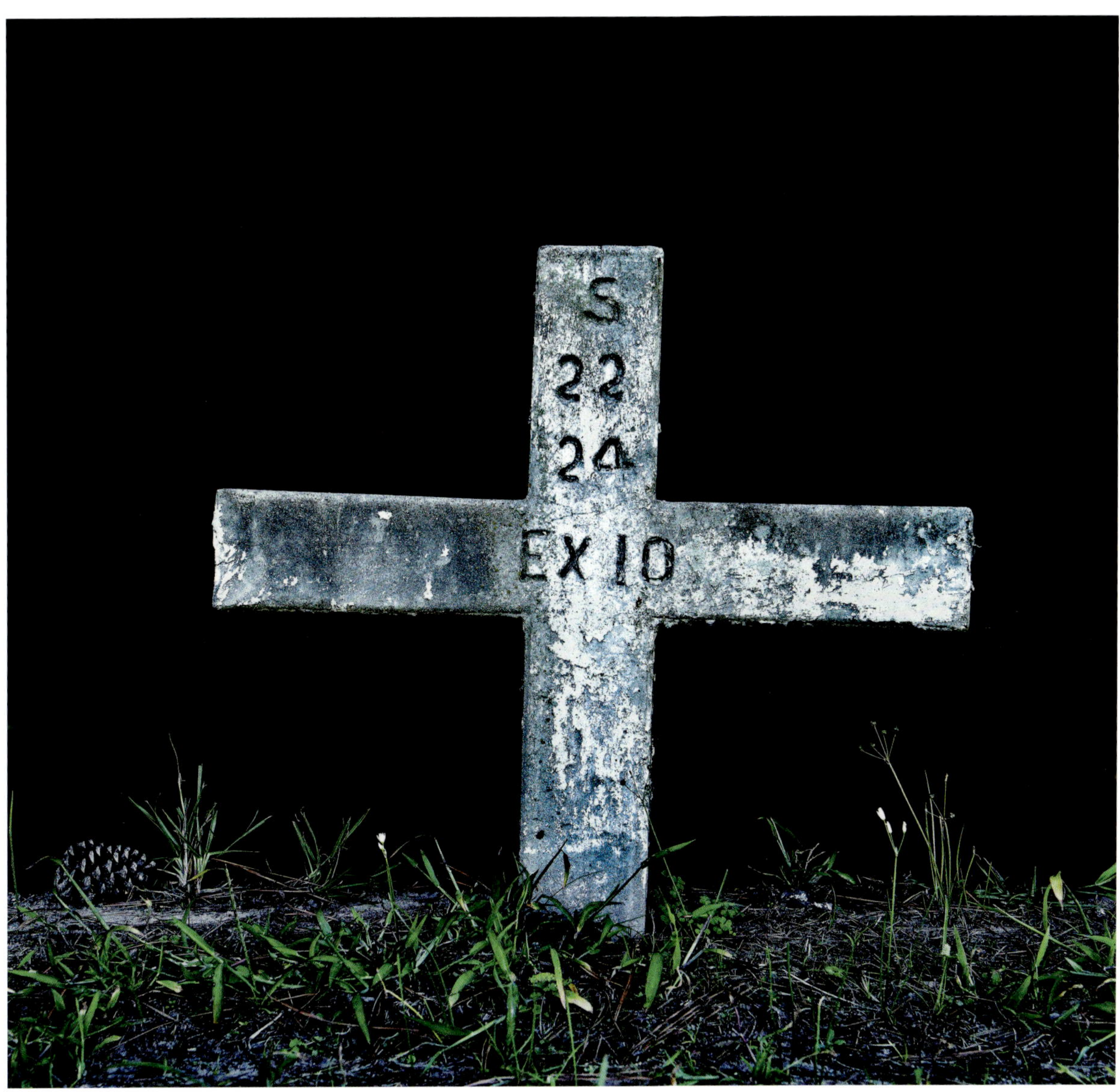

#148

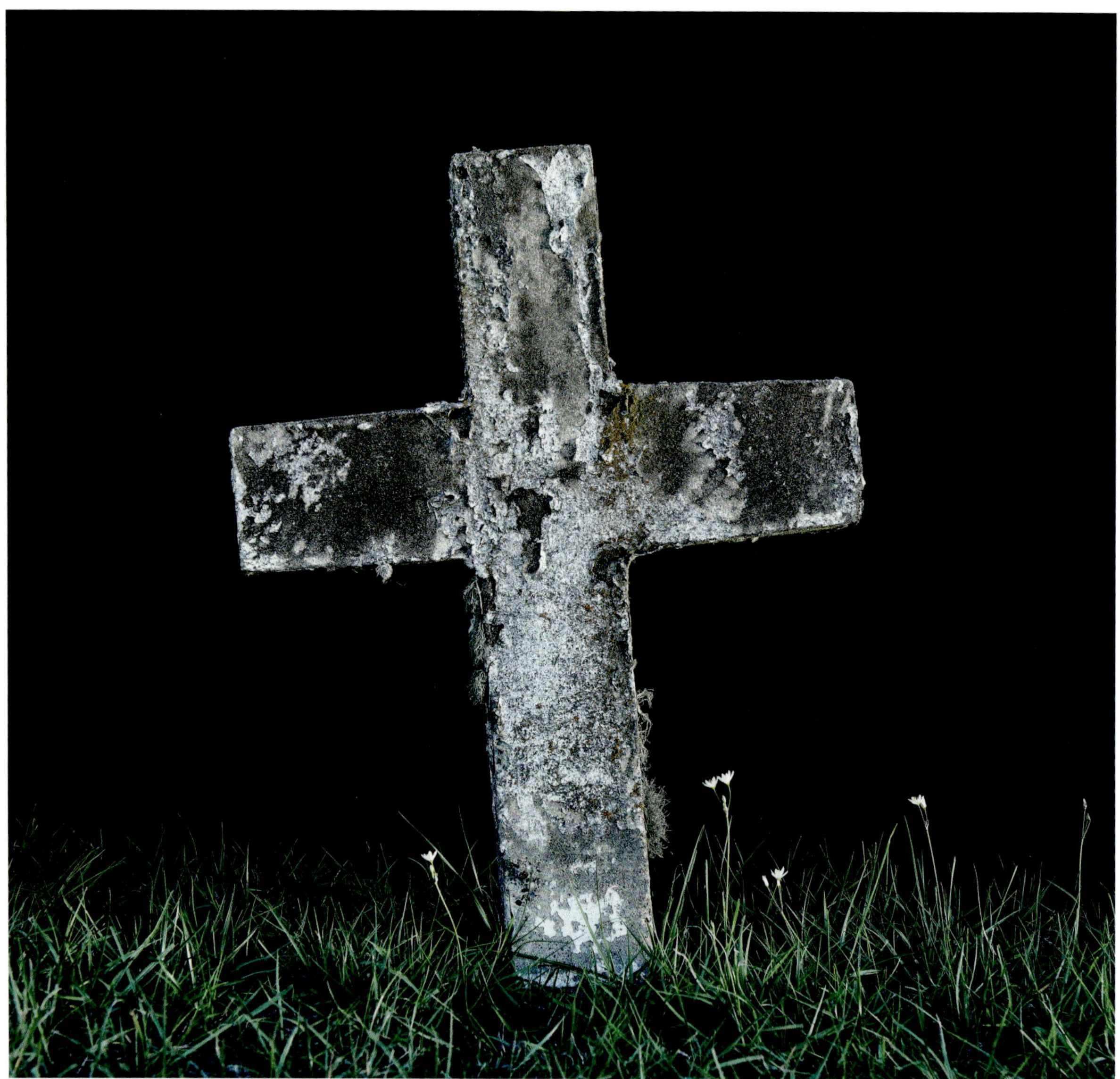

#177

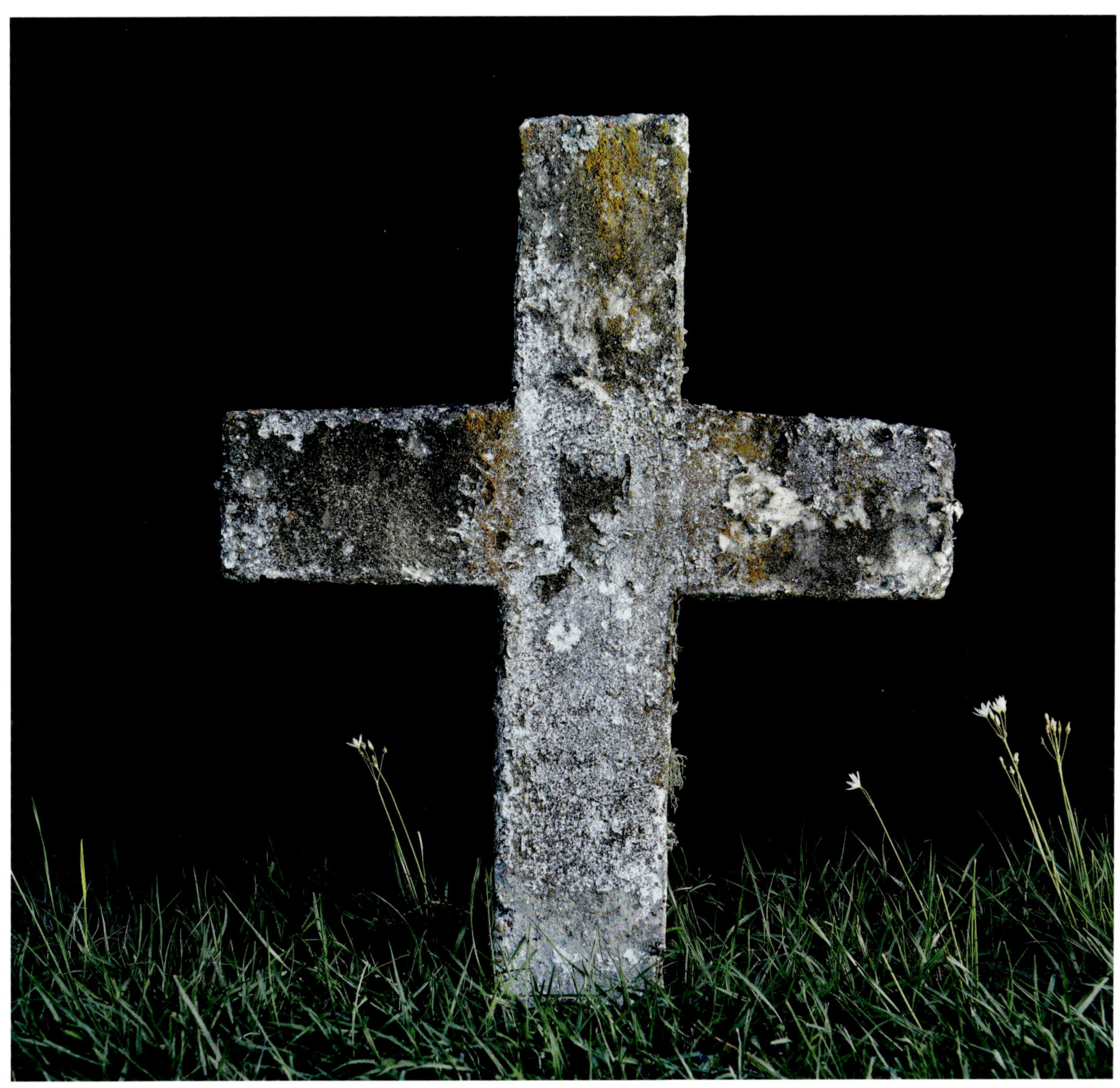

#176

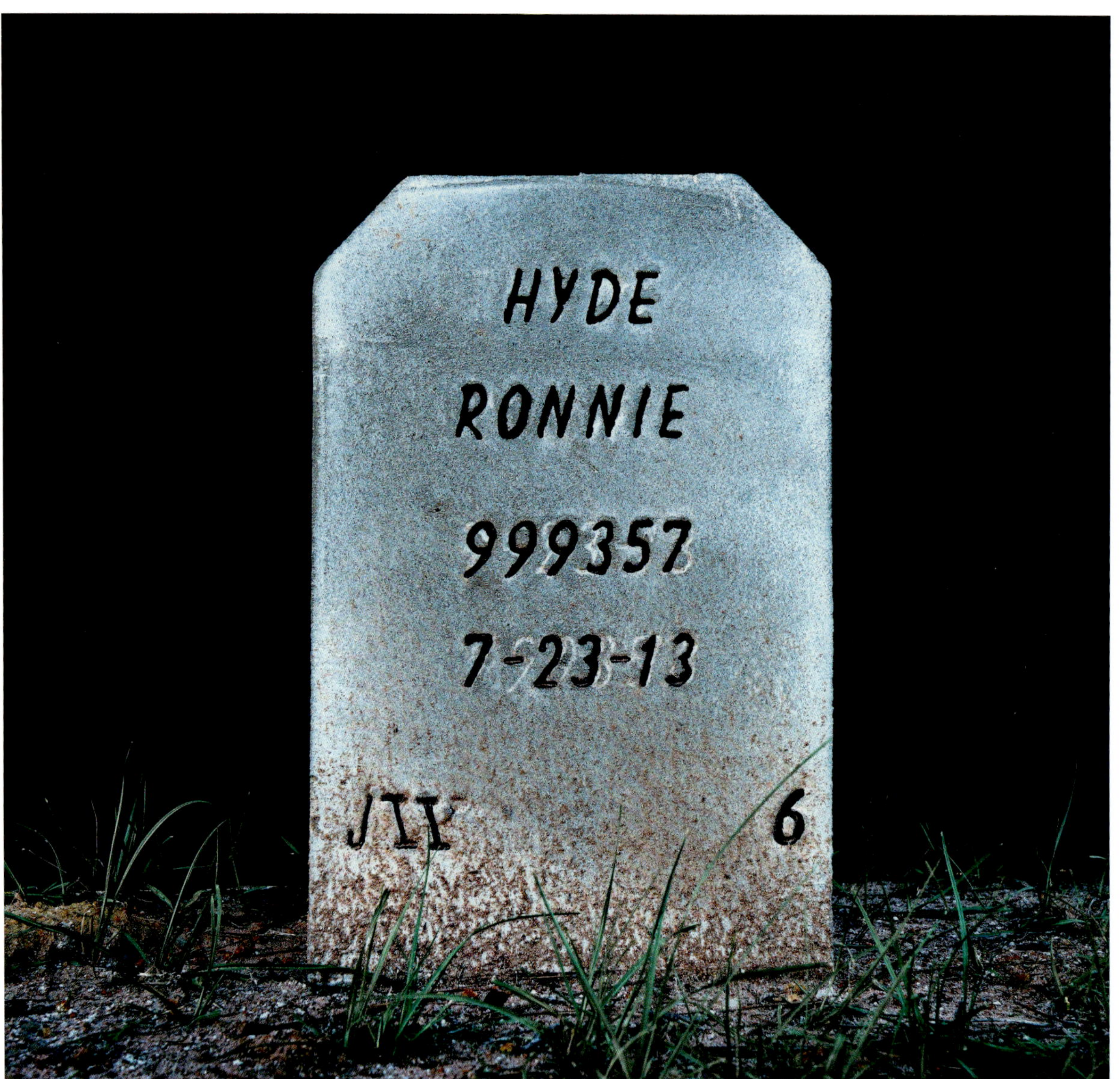

#076

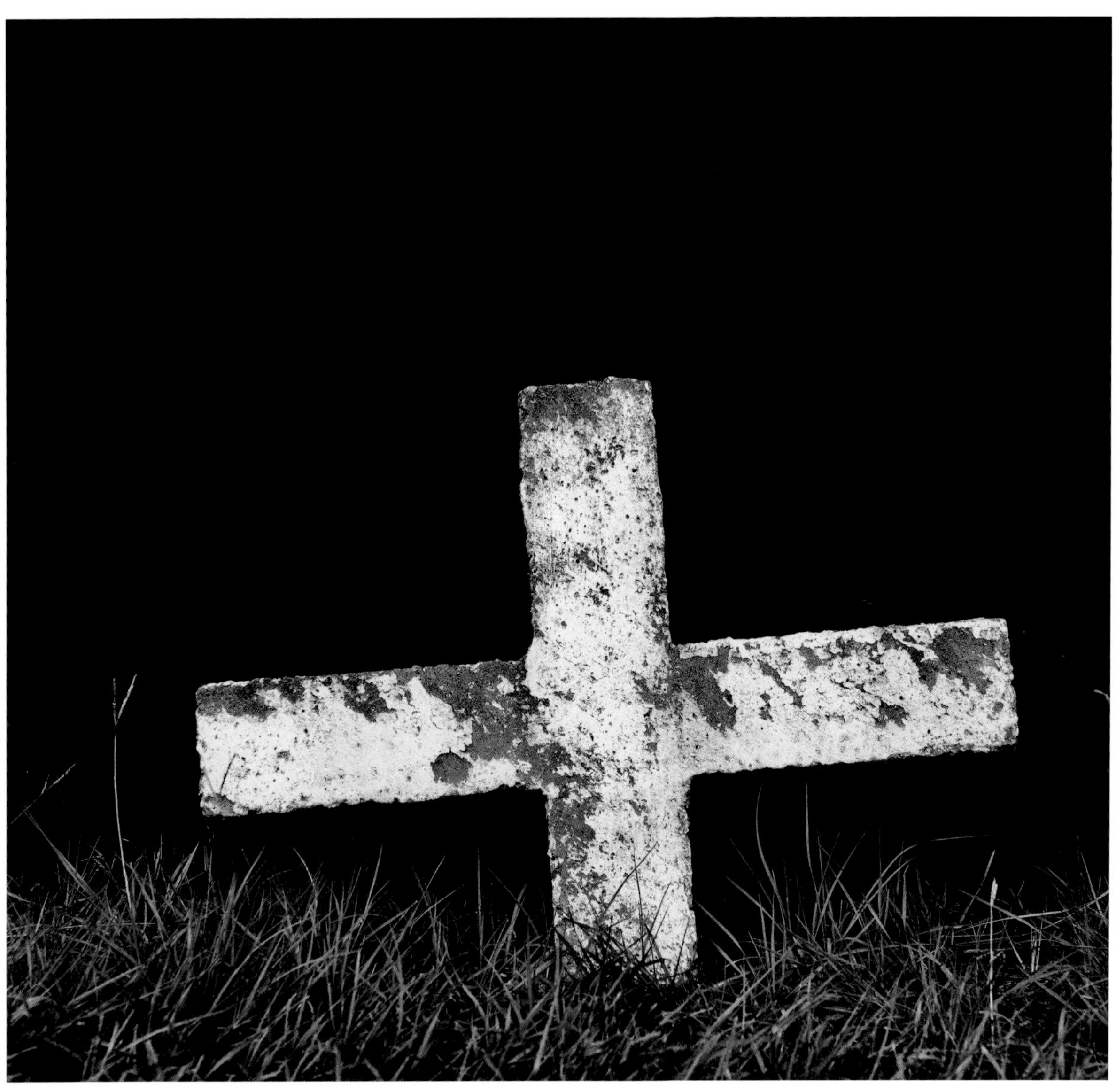

#171

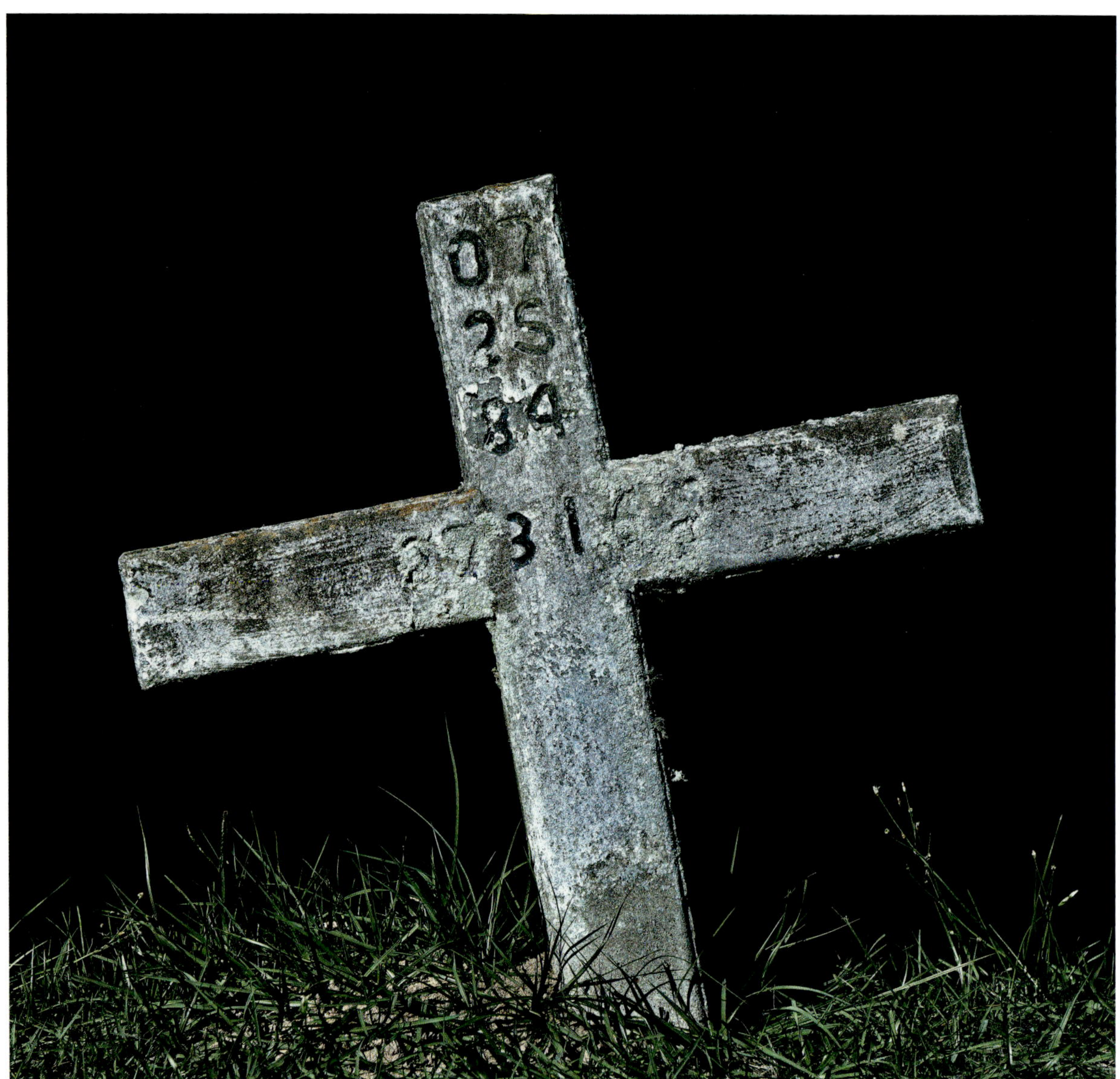

#180

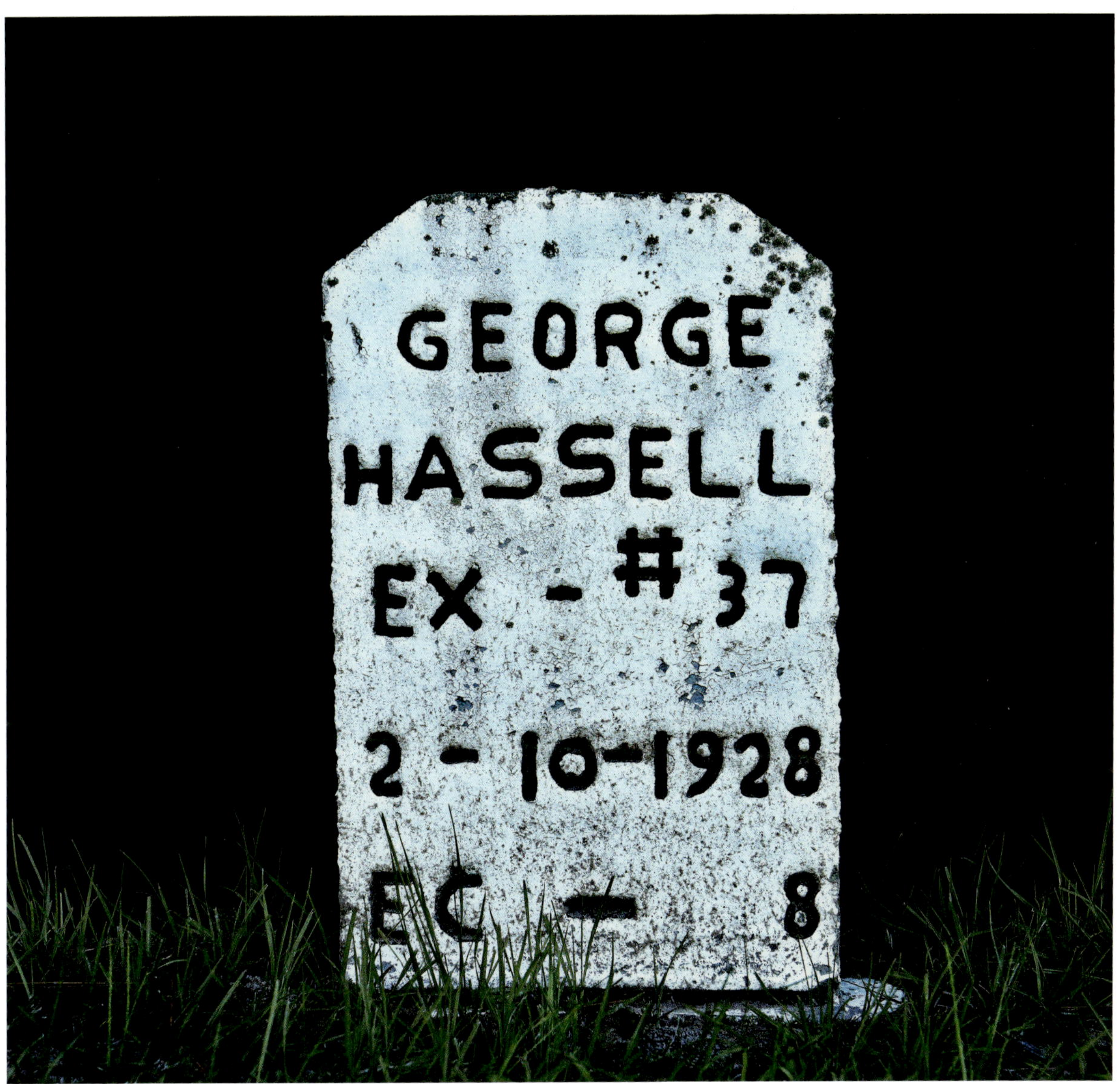

#006

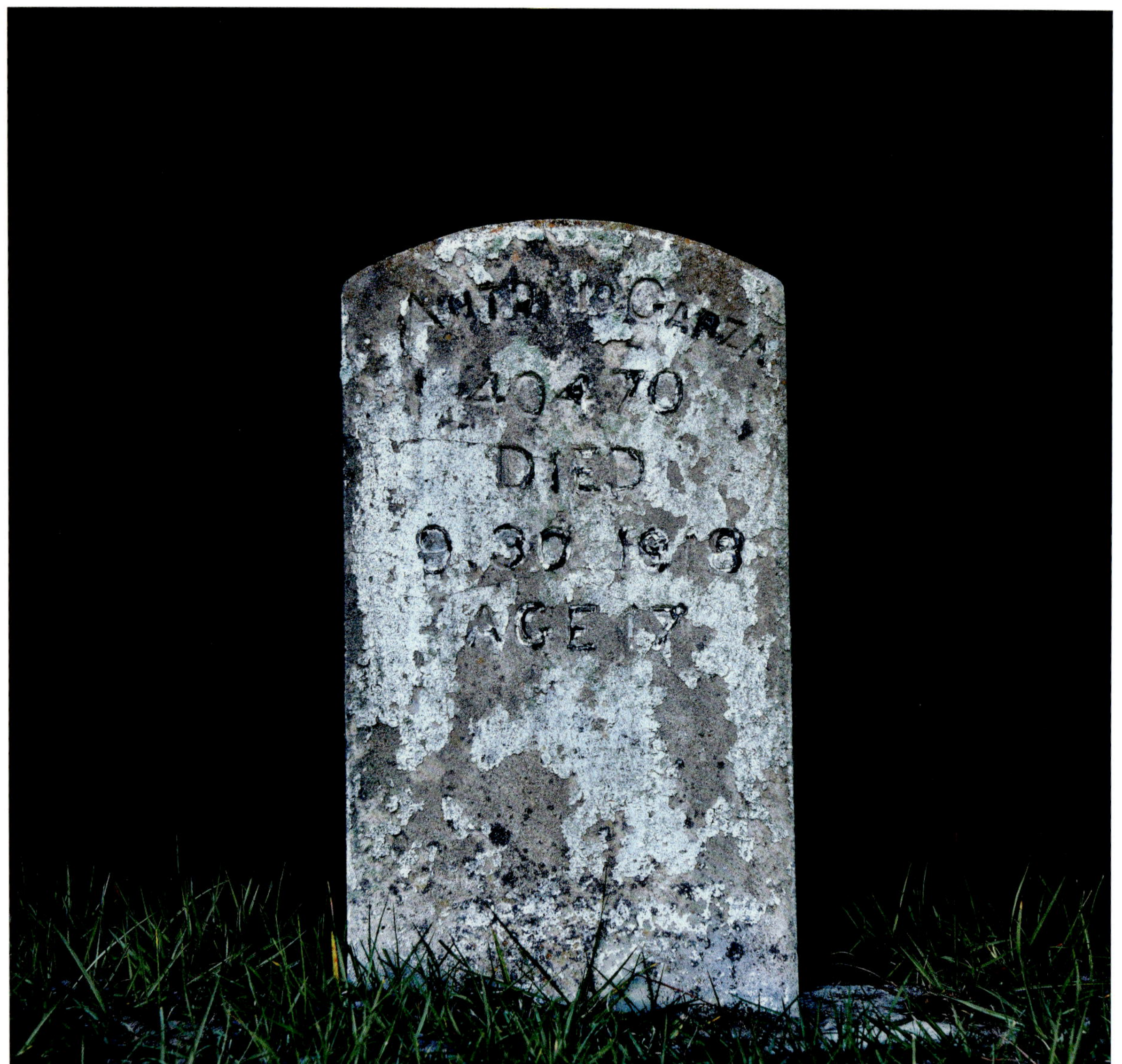

#081

DERRICK
O'BRIEN
999131
.06
K. F. II
My command is this:
Love each other as
I have loved you
John15:12
Love

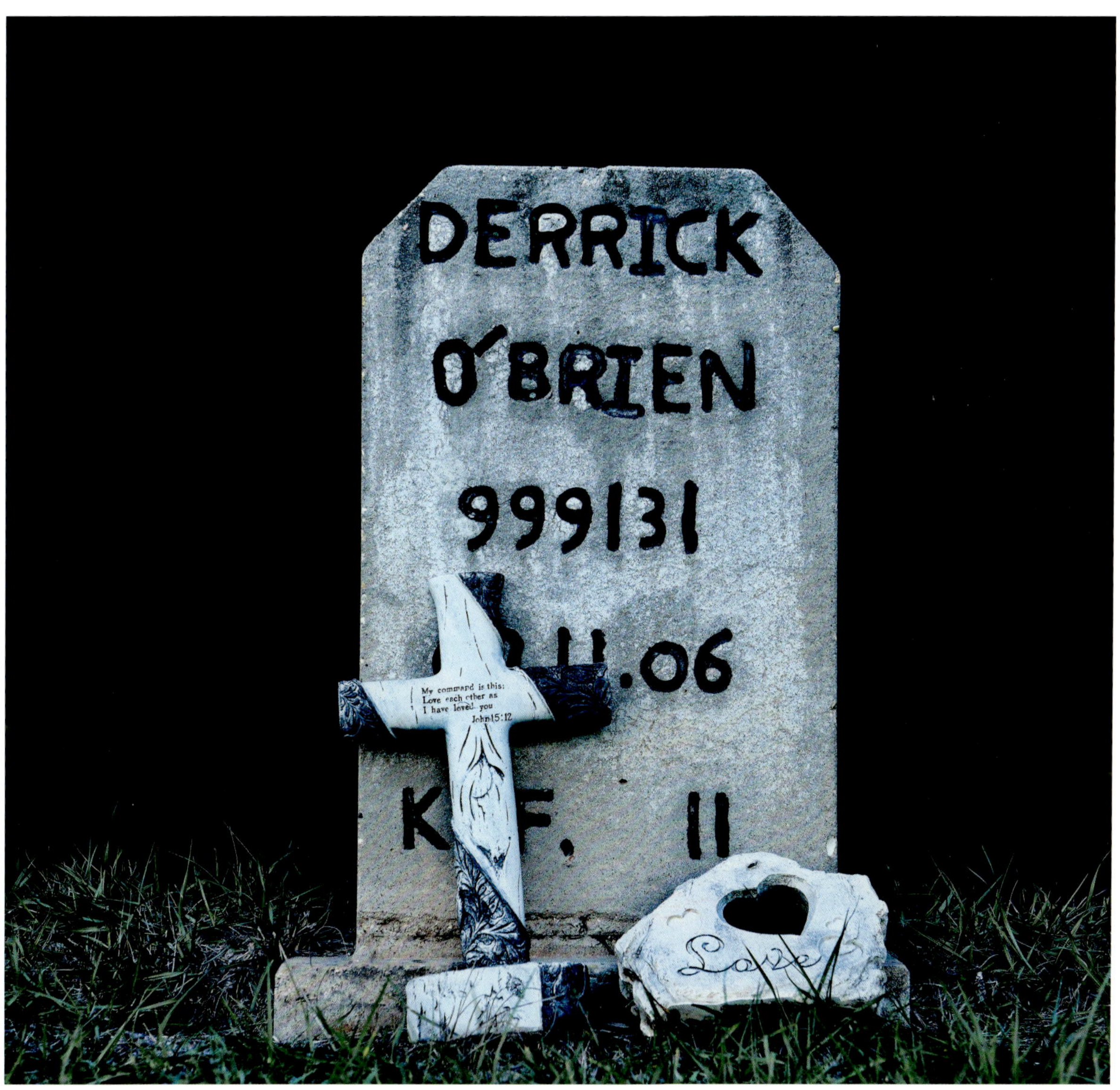

#093

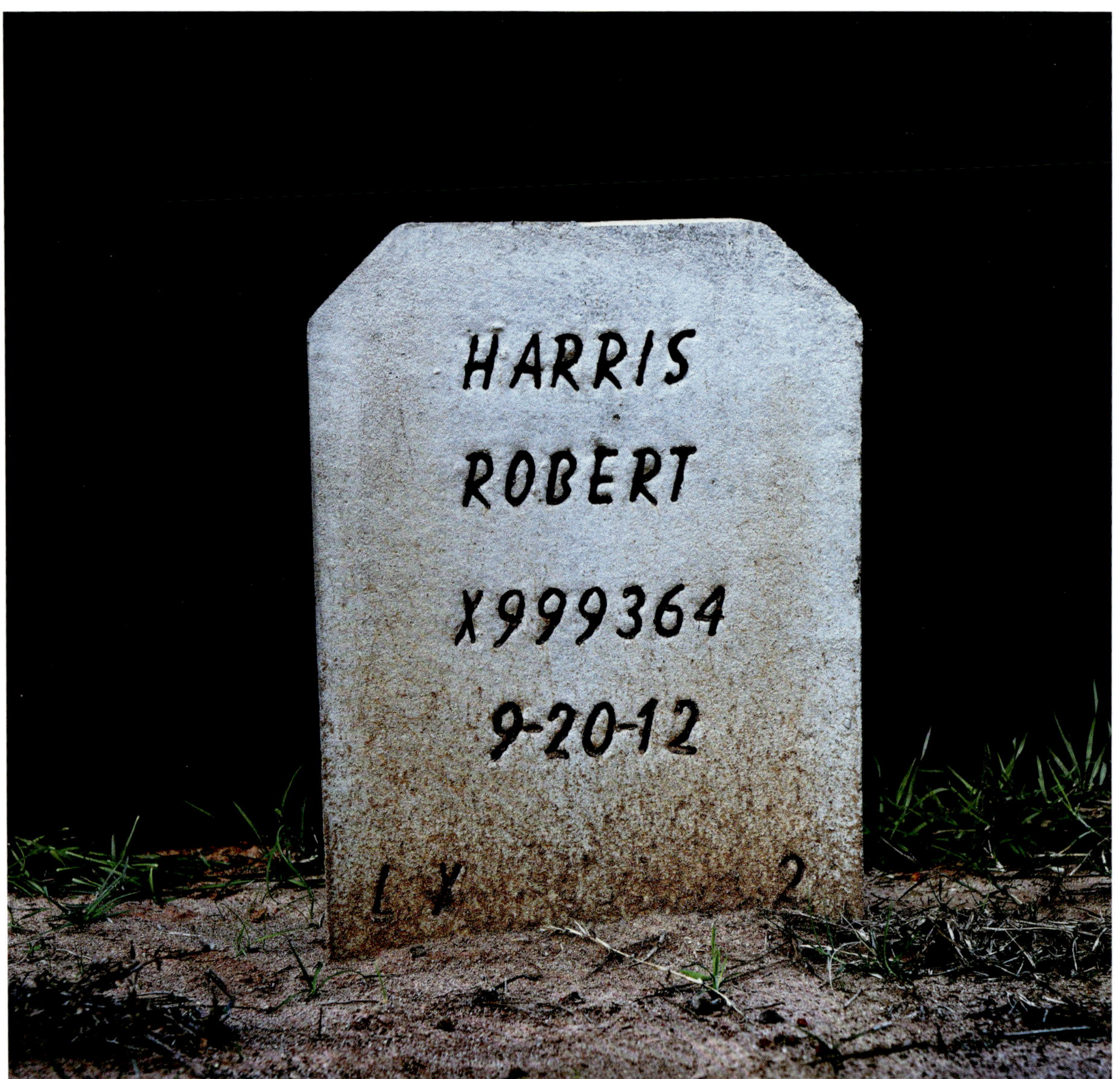

#103

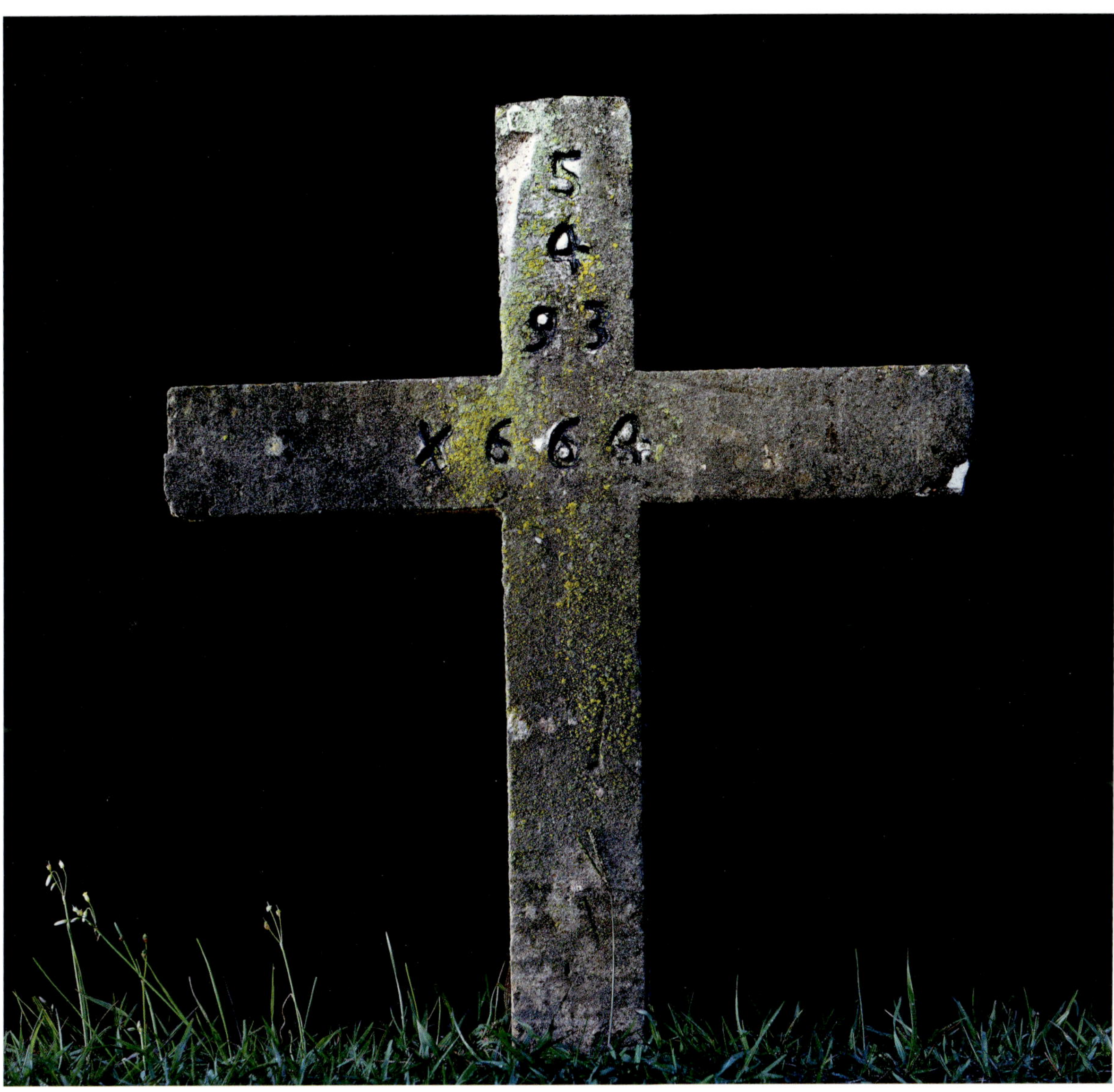

#015

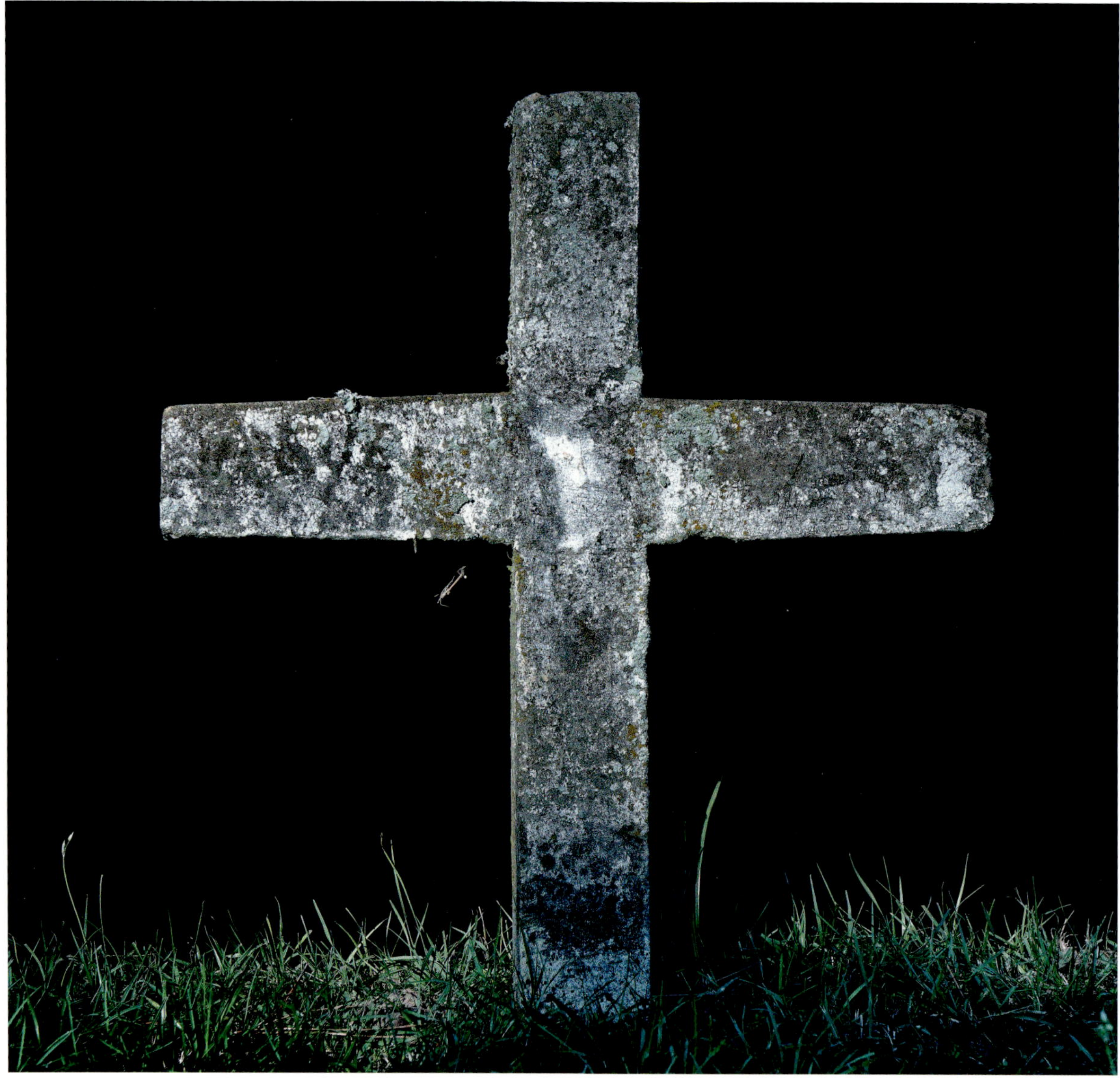

#168

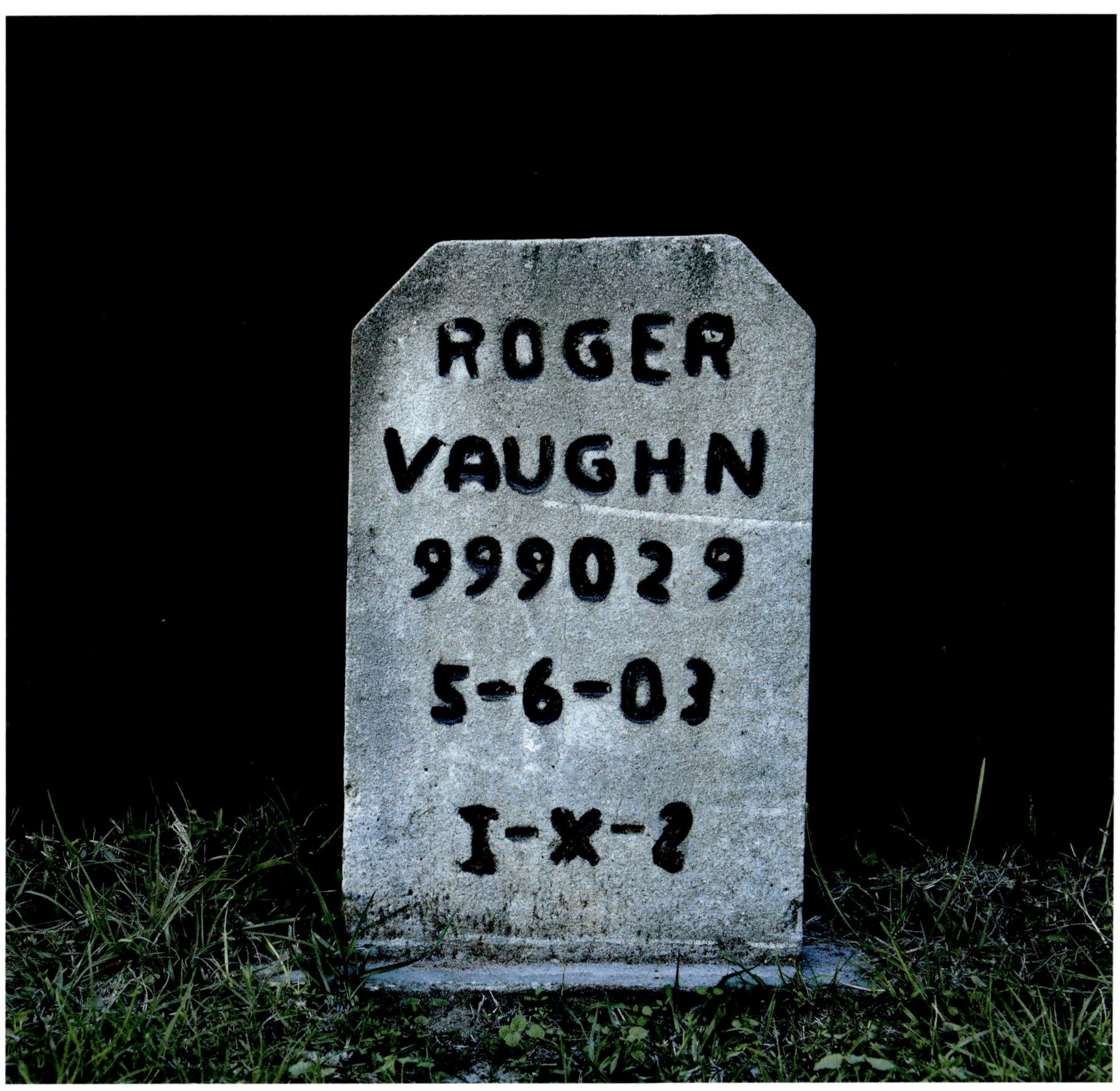

#074

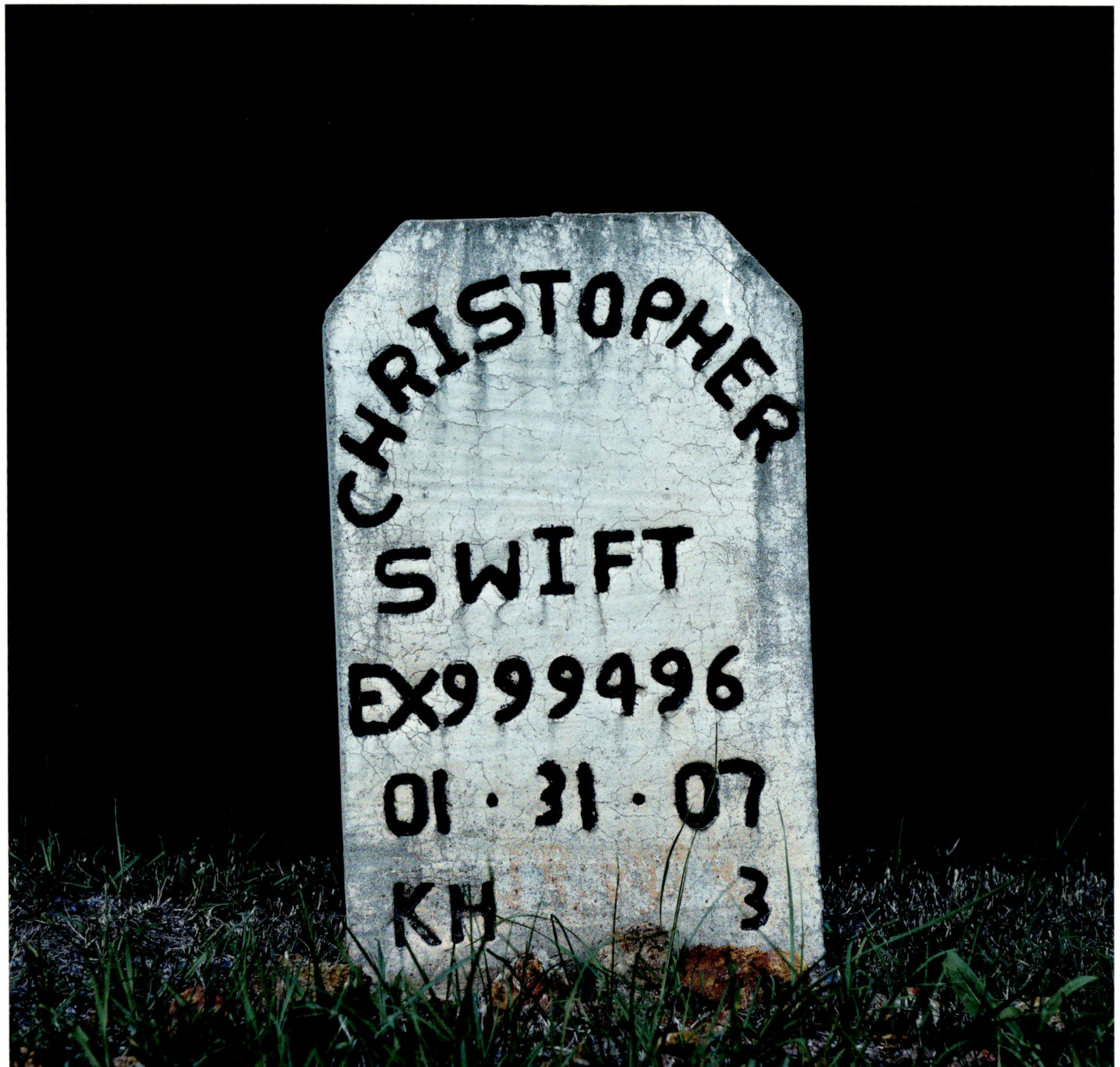

CHRISTOPHER
SWIFT
EX999496
01 · 31 · 07
KH   3

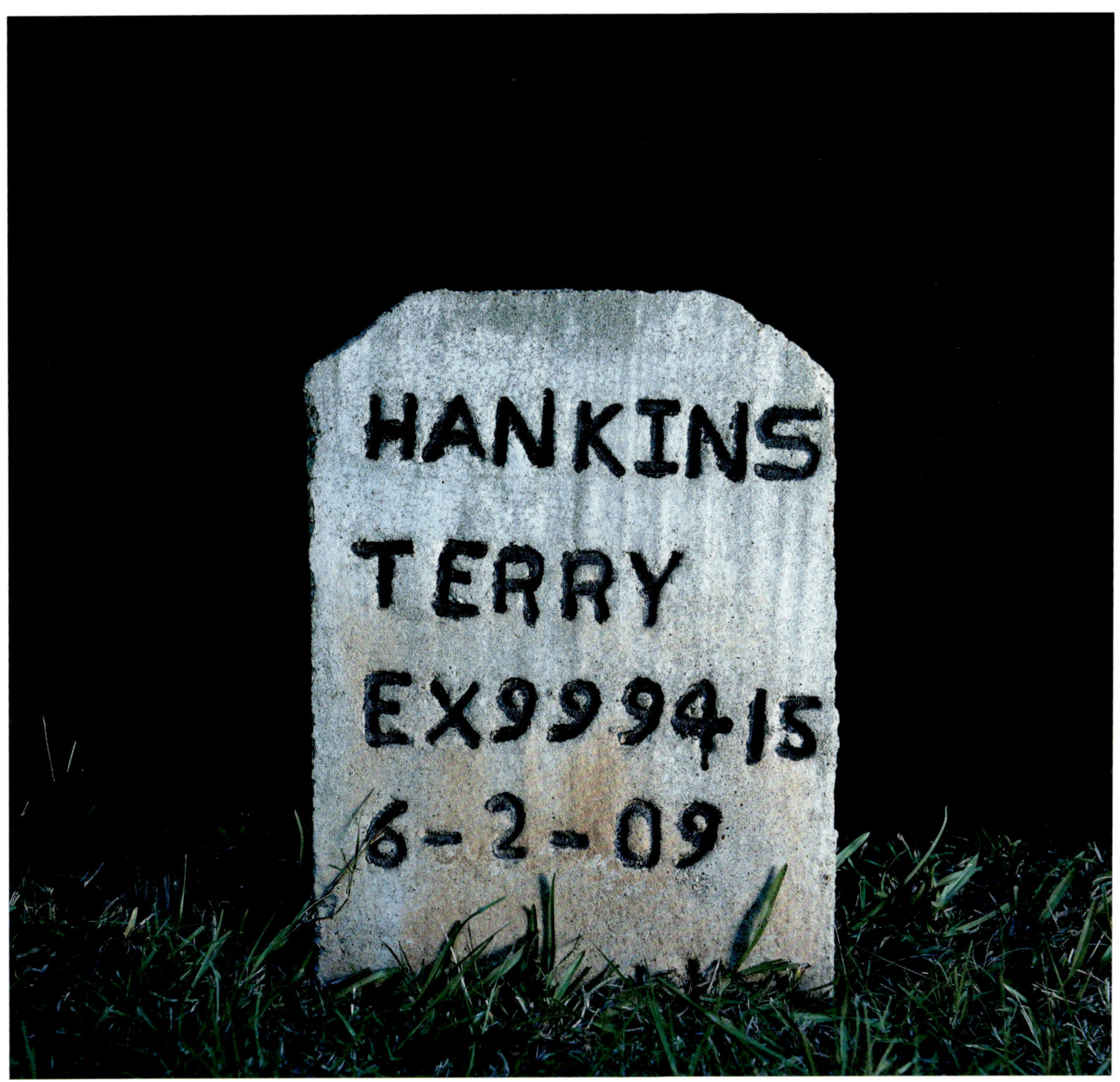

#106

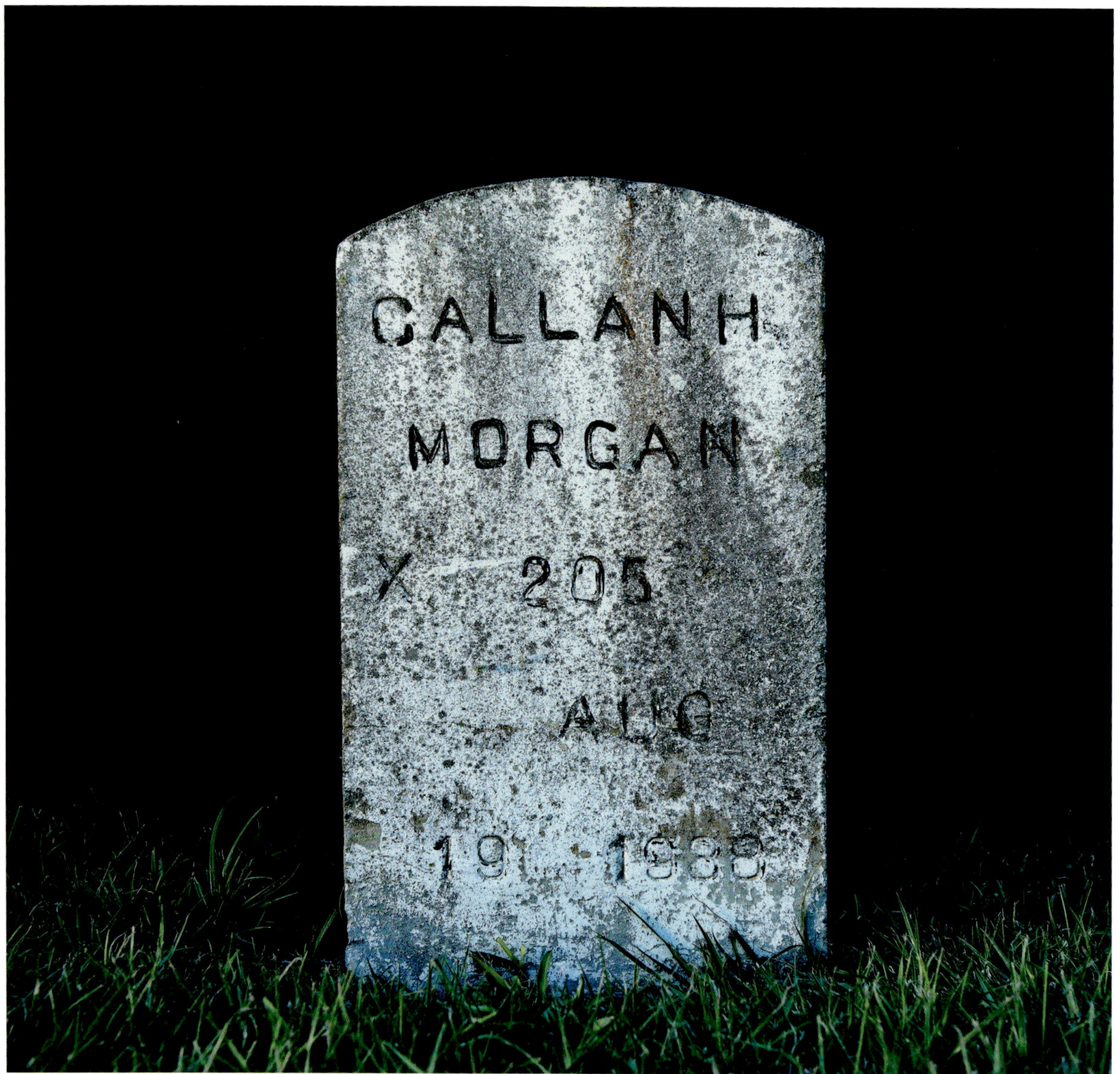

#114

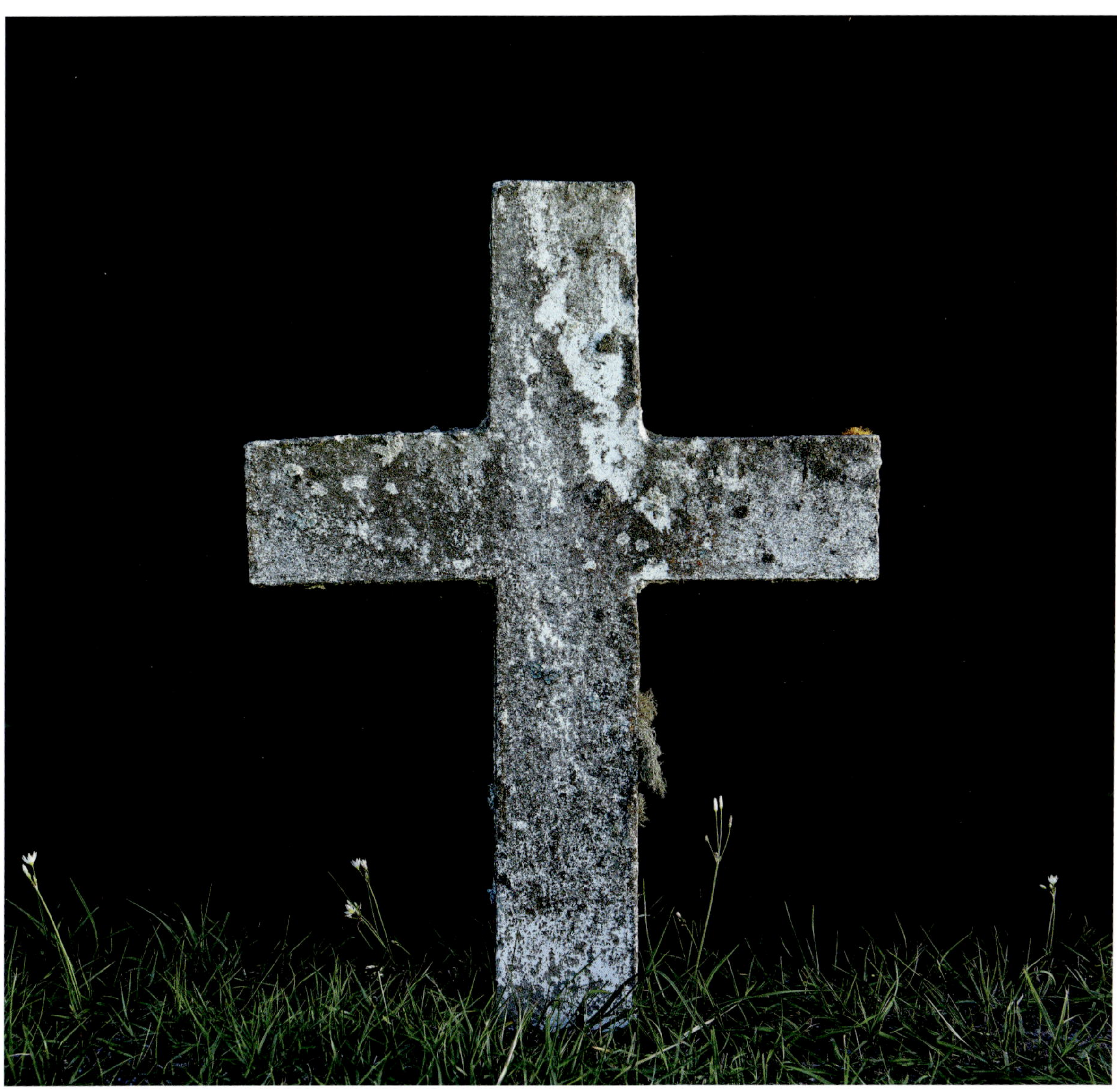

#178

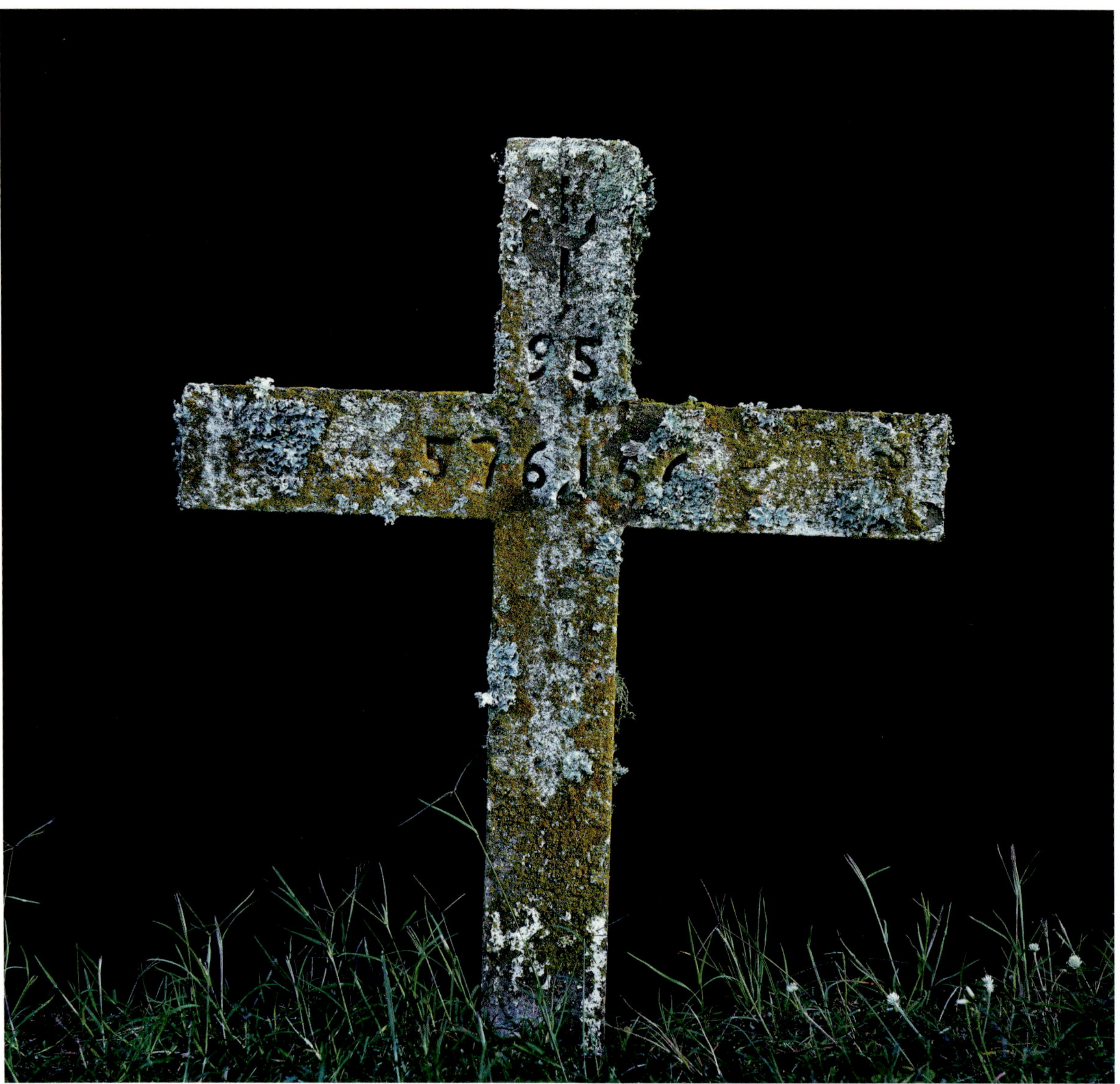

#125

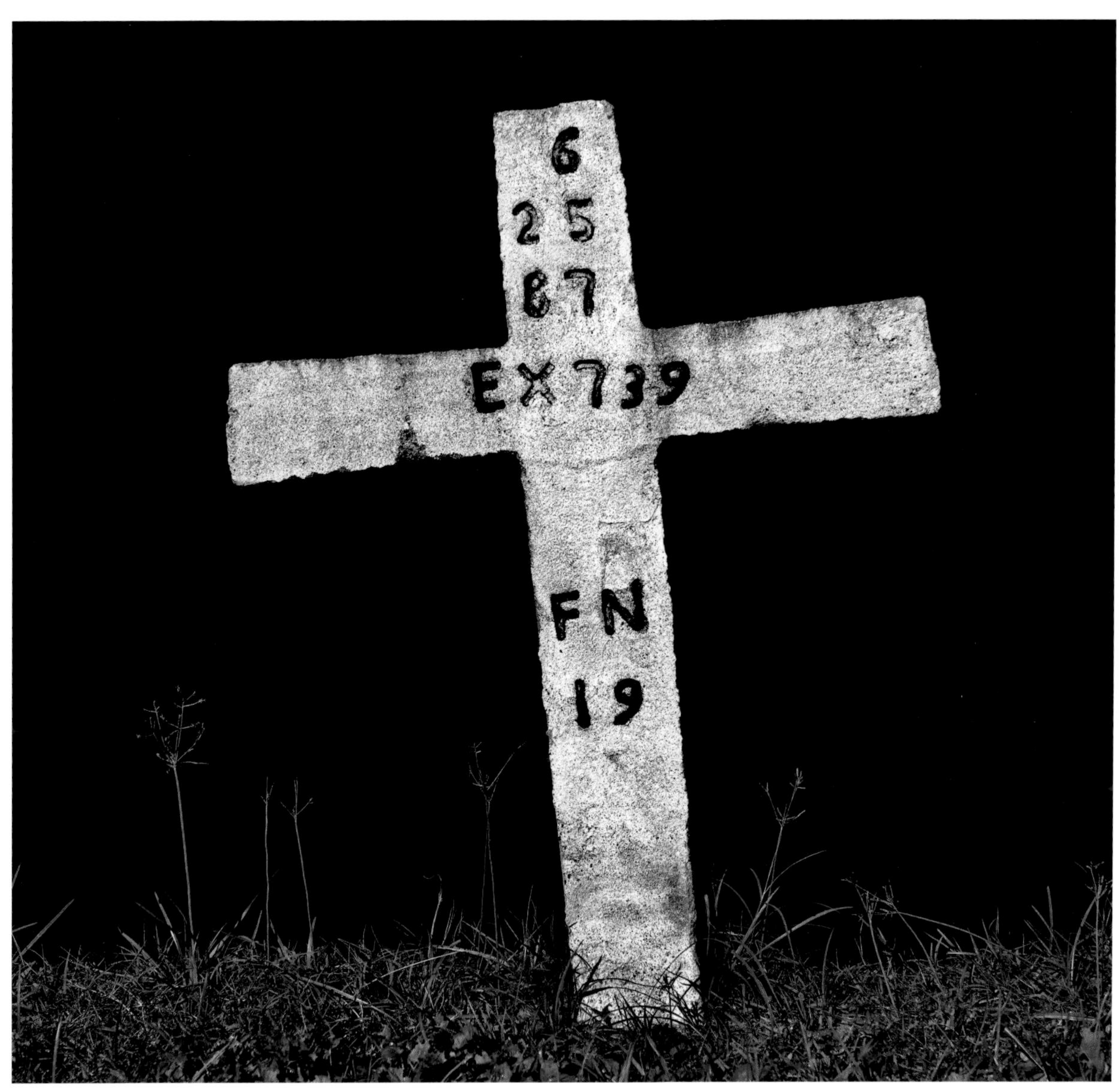

#029

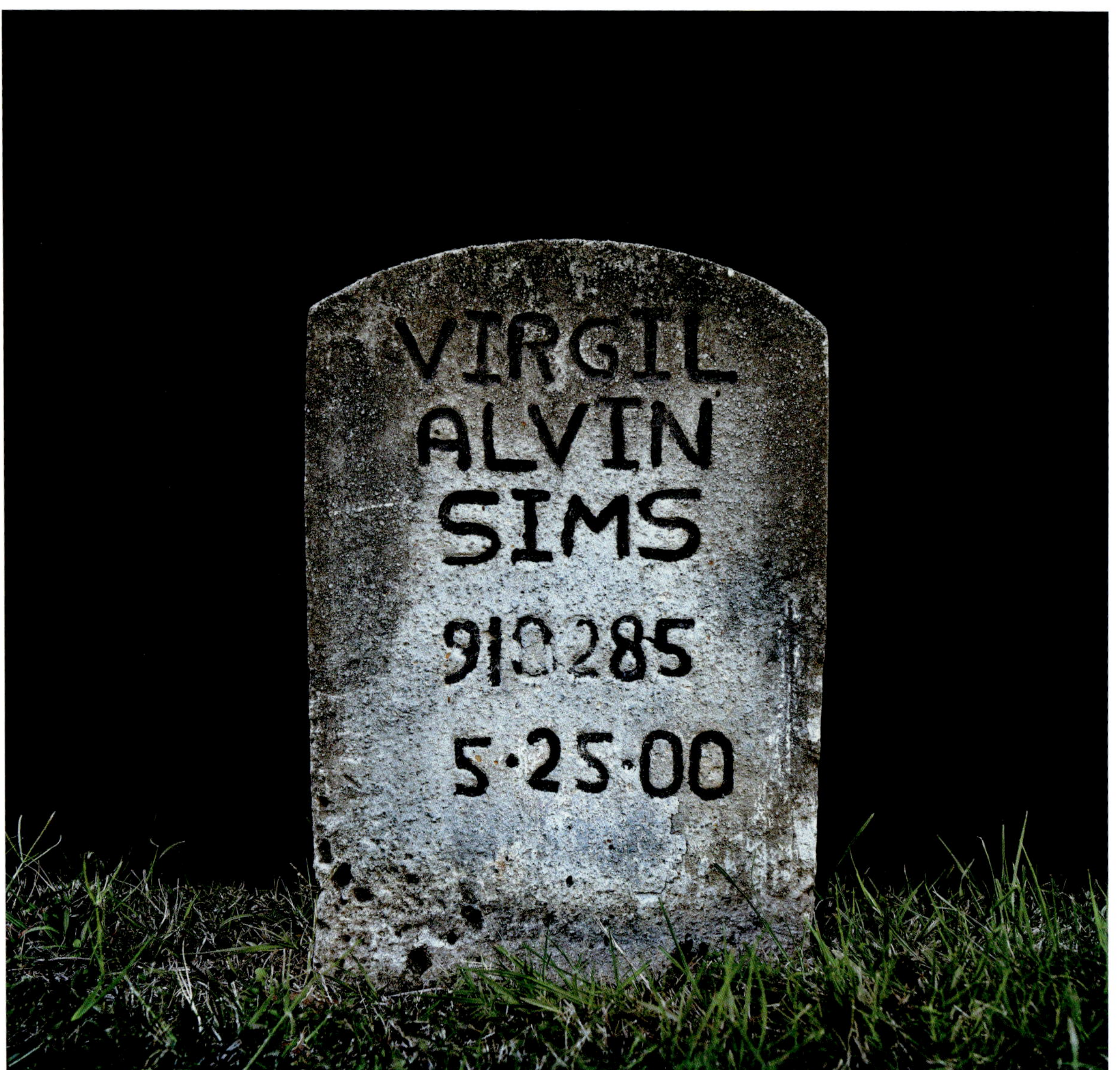

#057

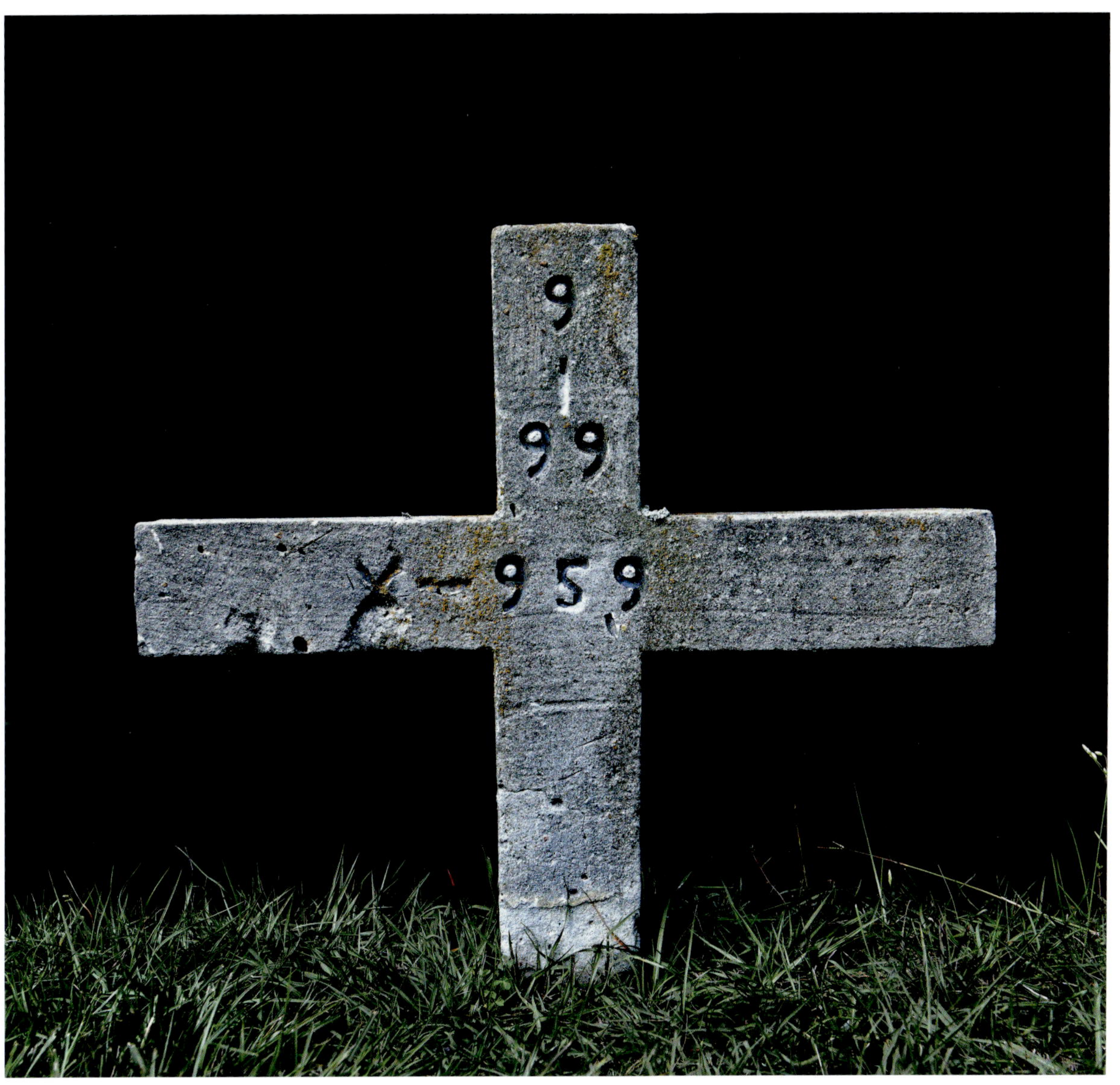

#118

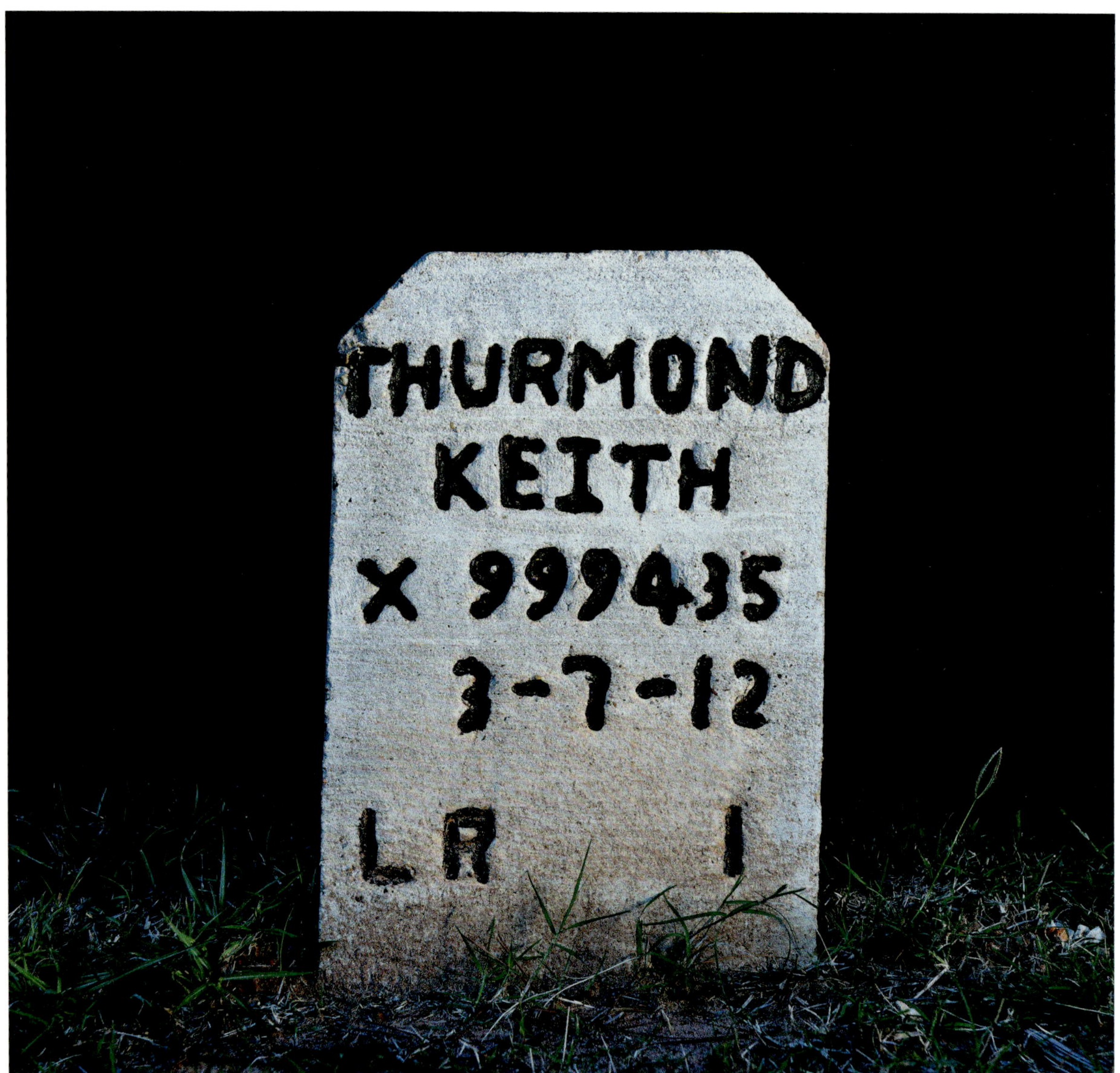

#102

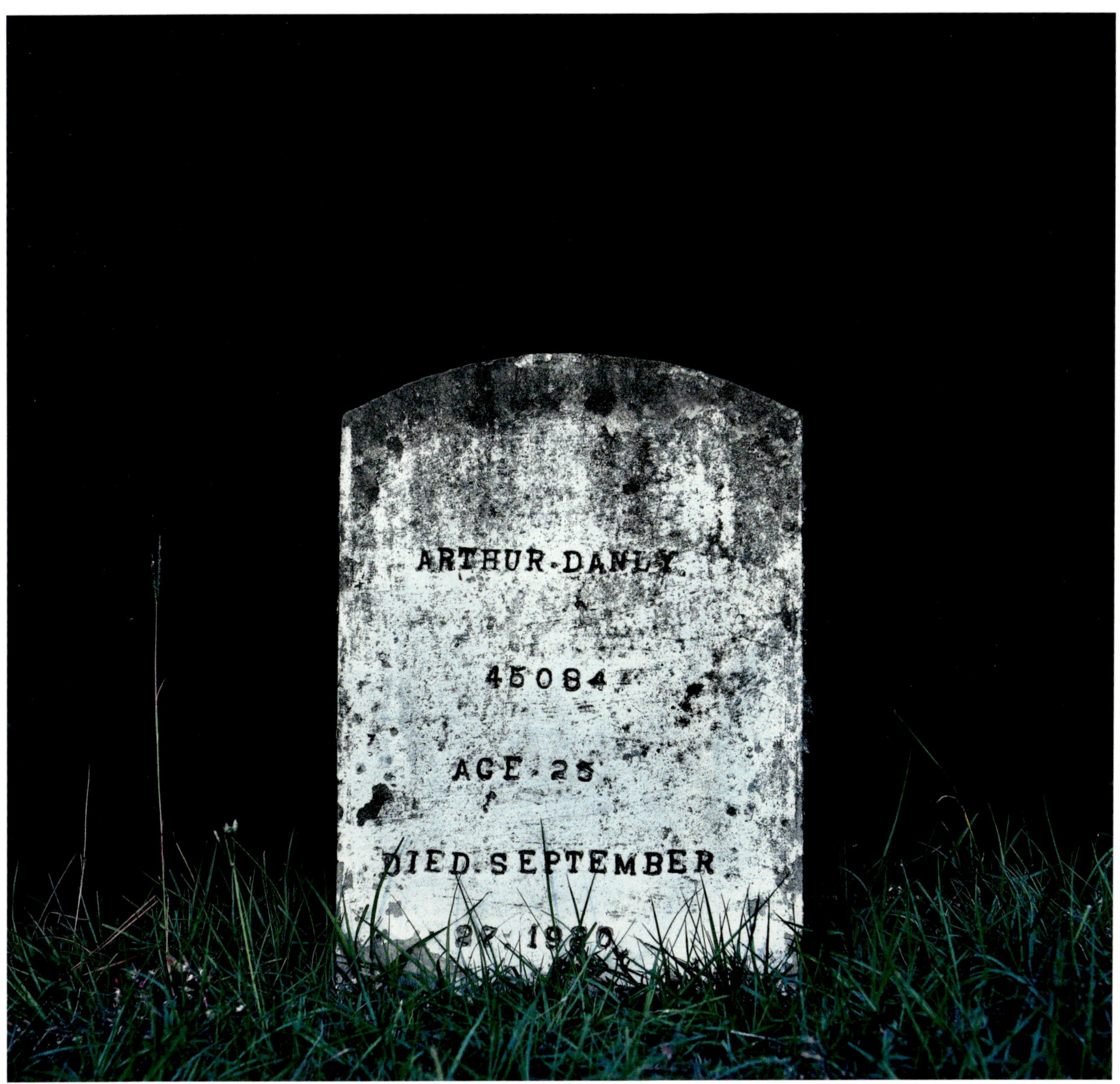

#087

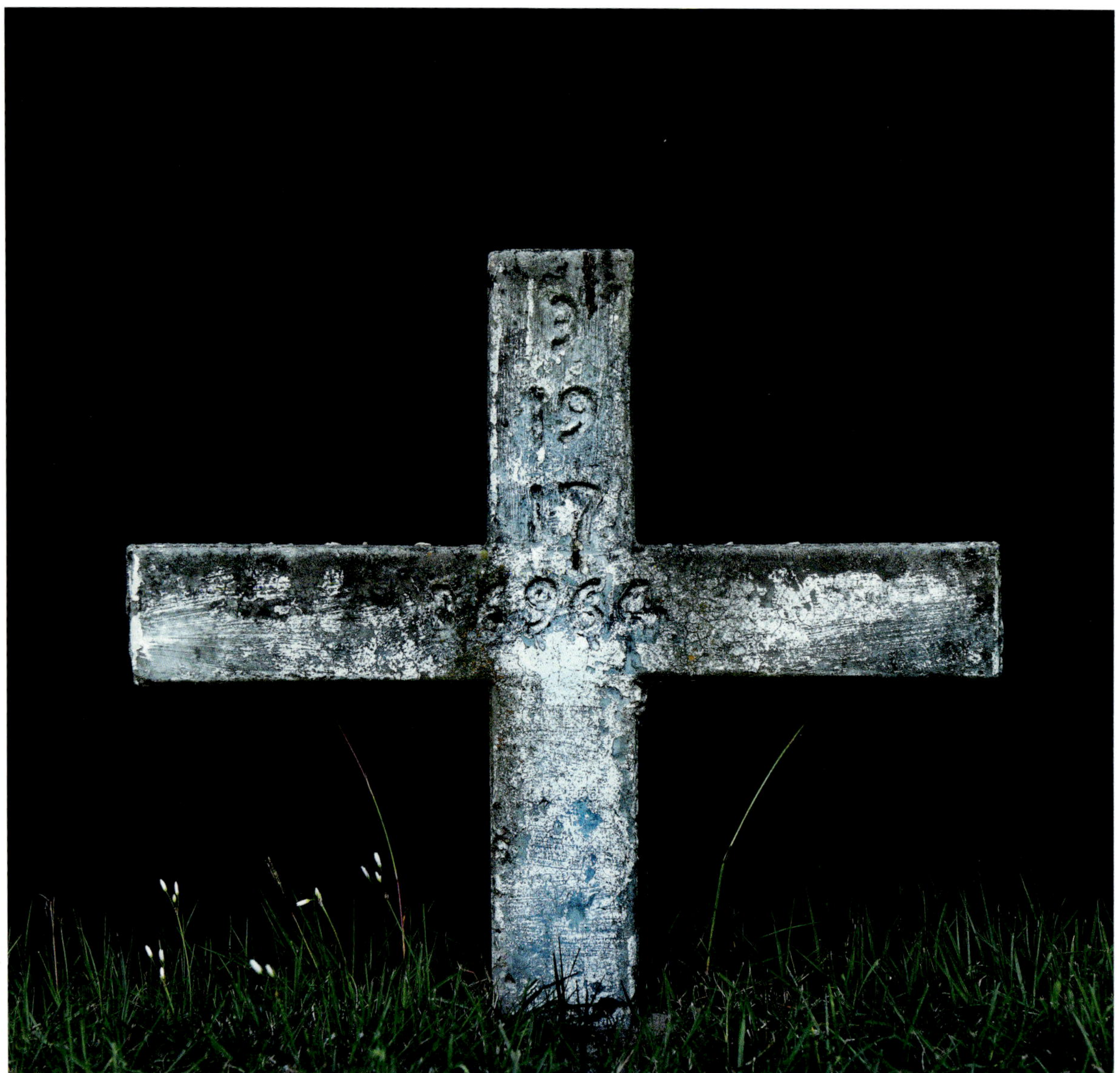

#150

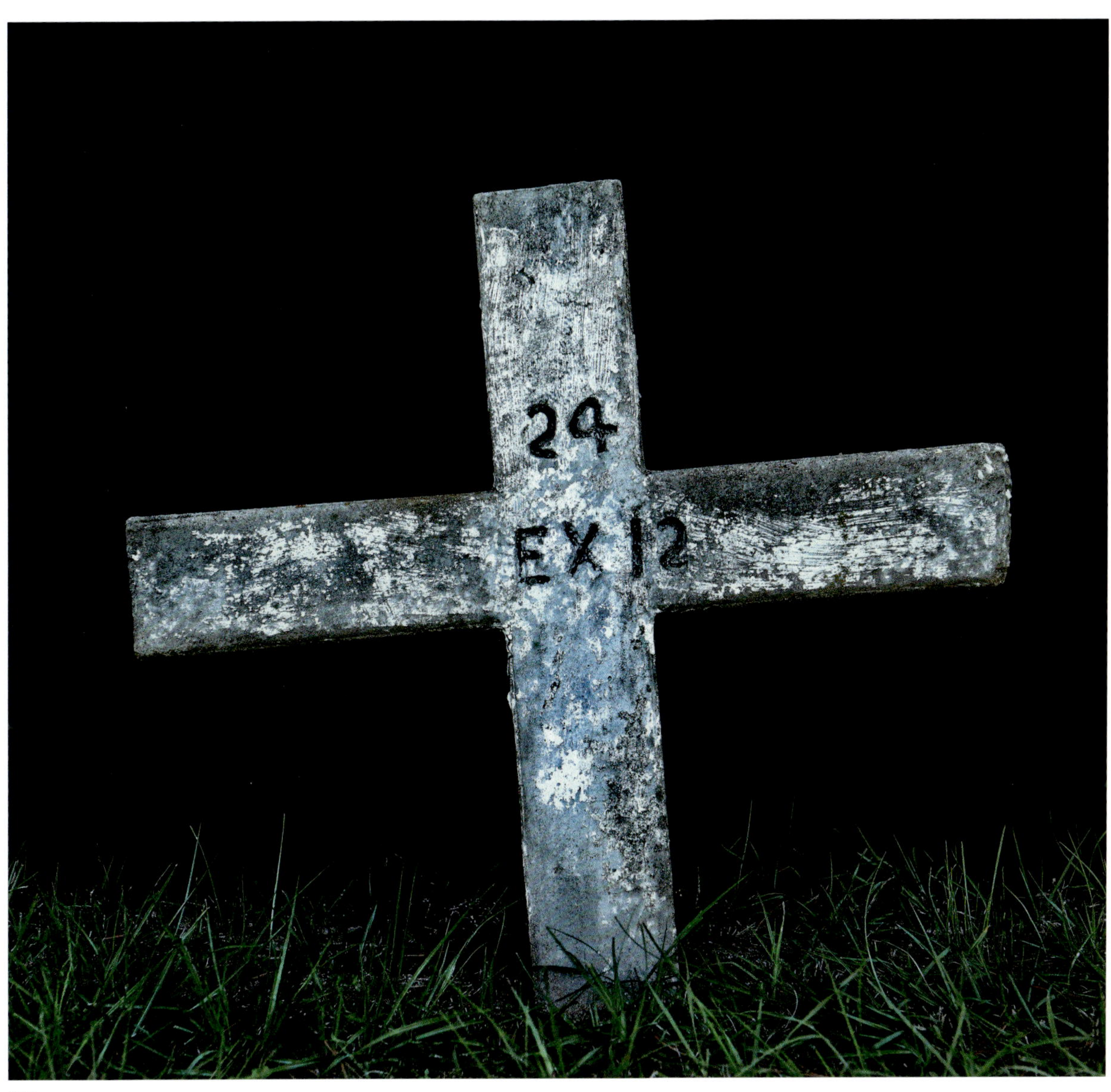

#050

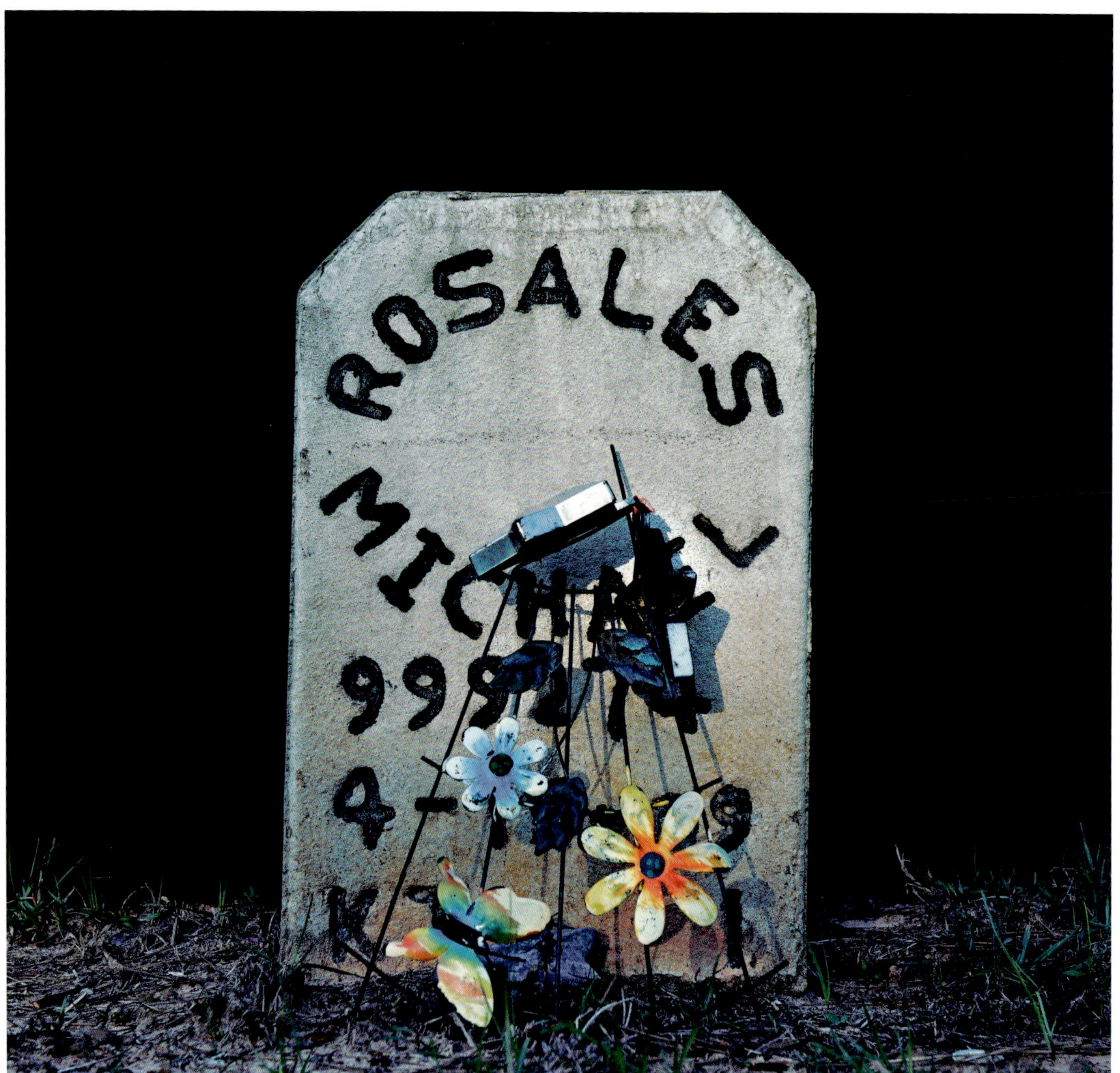

#100

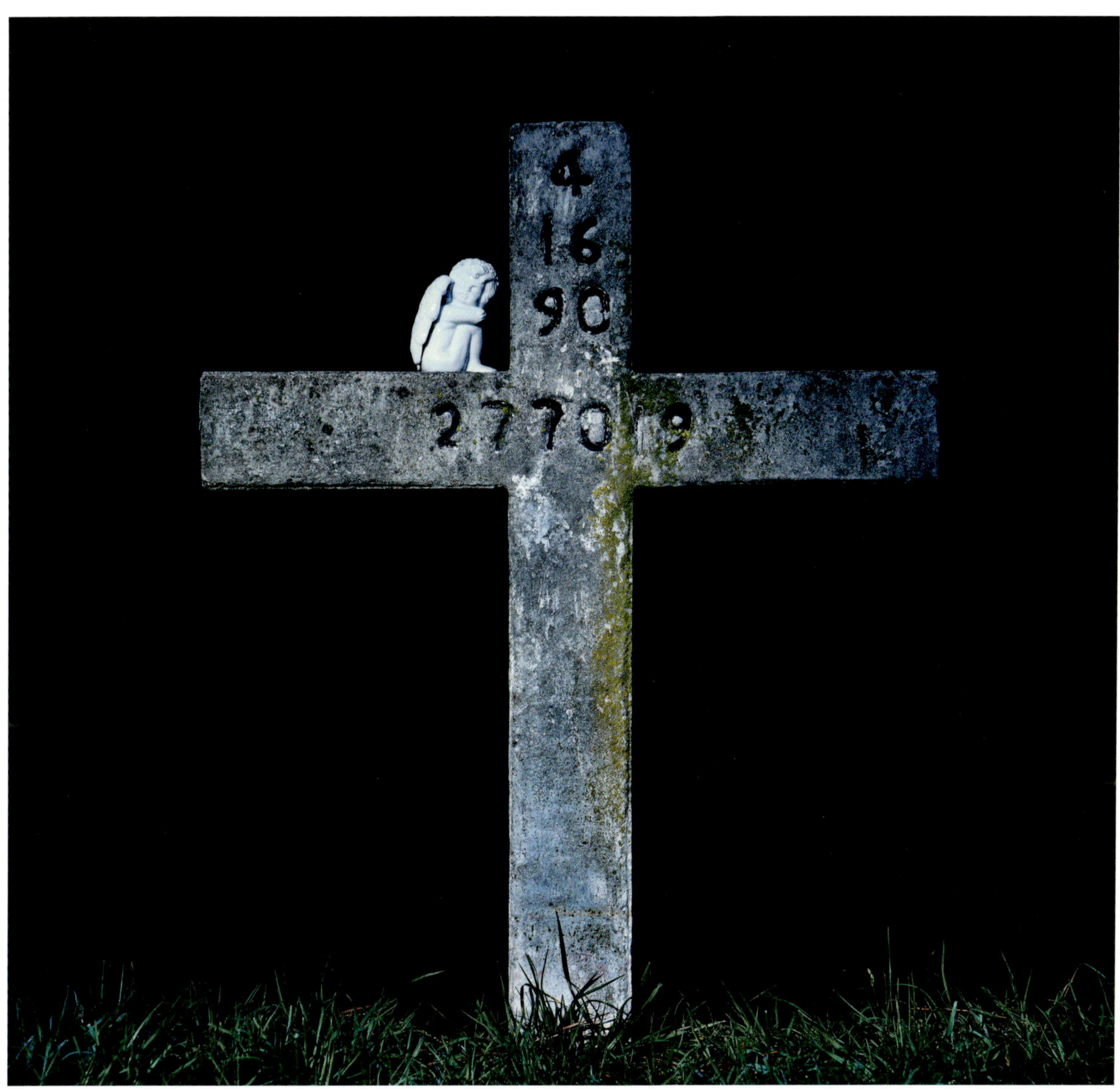

#022

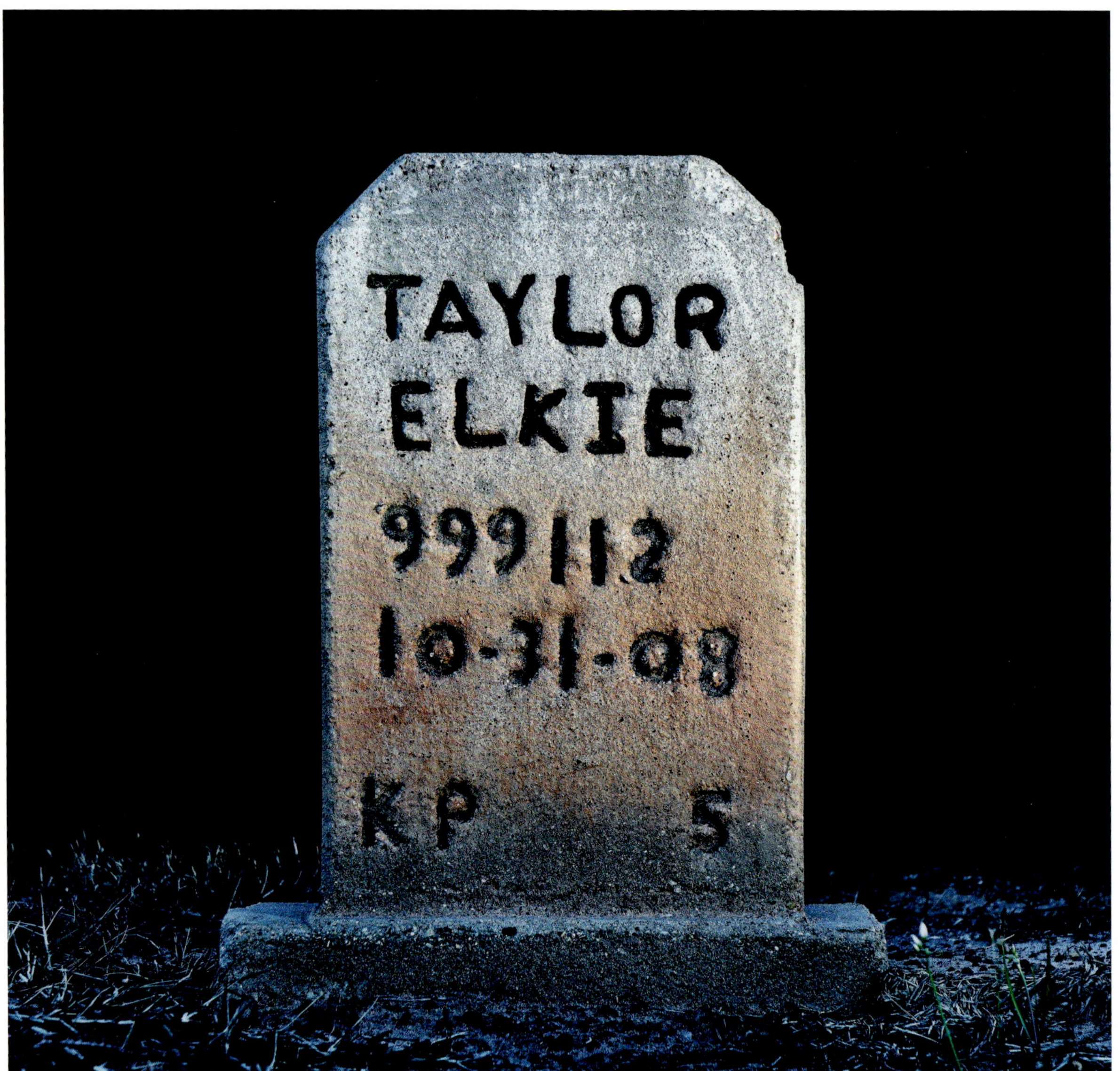

#099

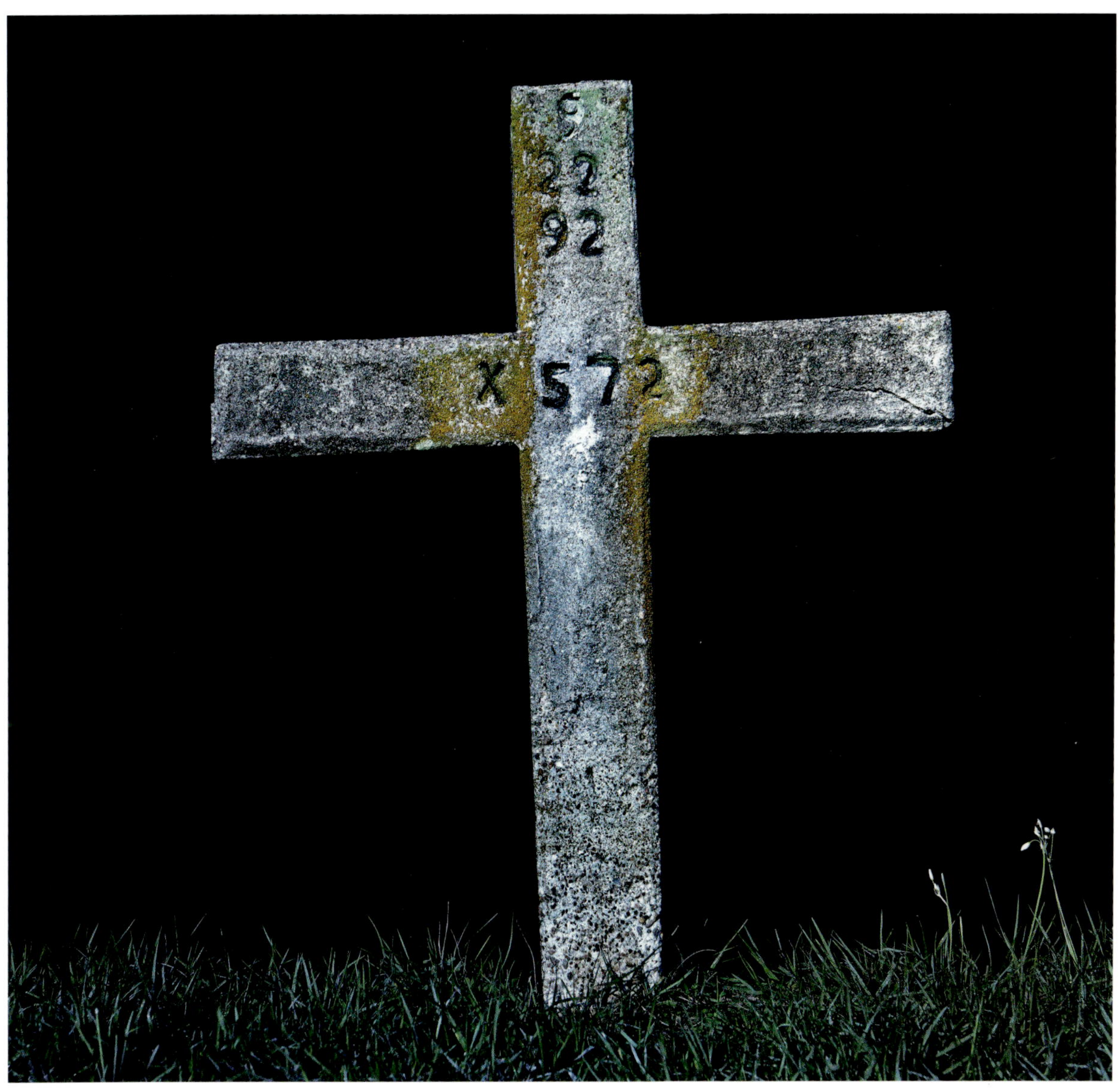

#142

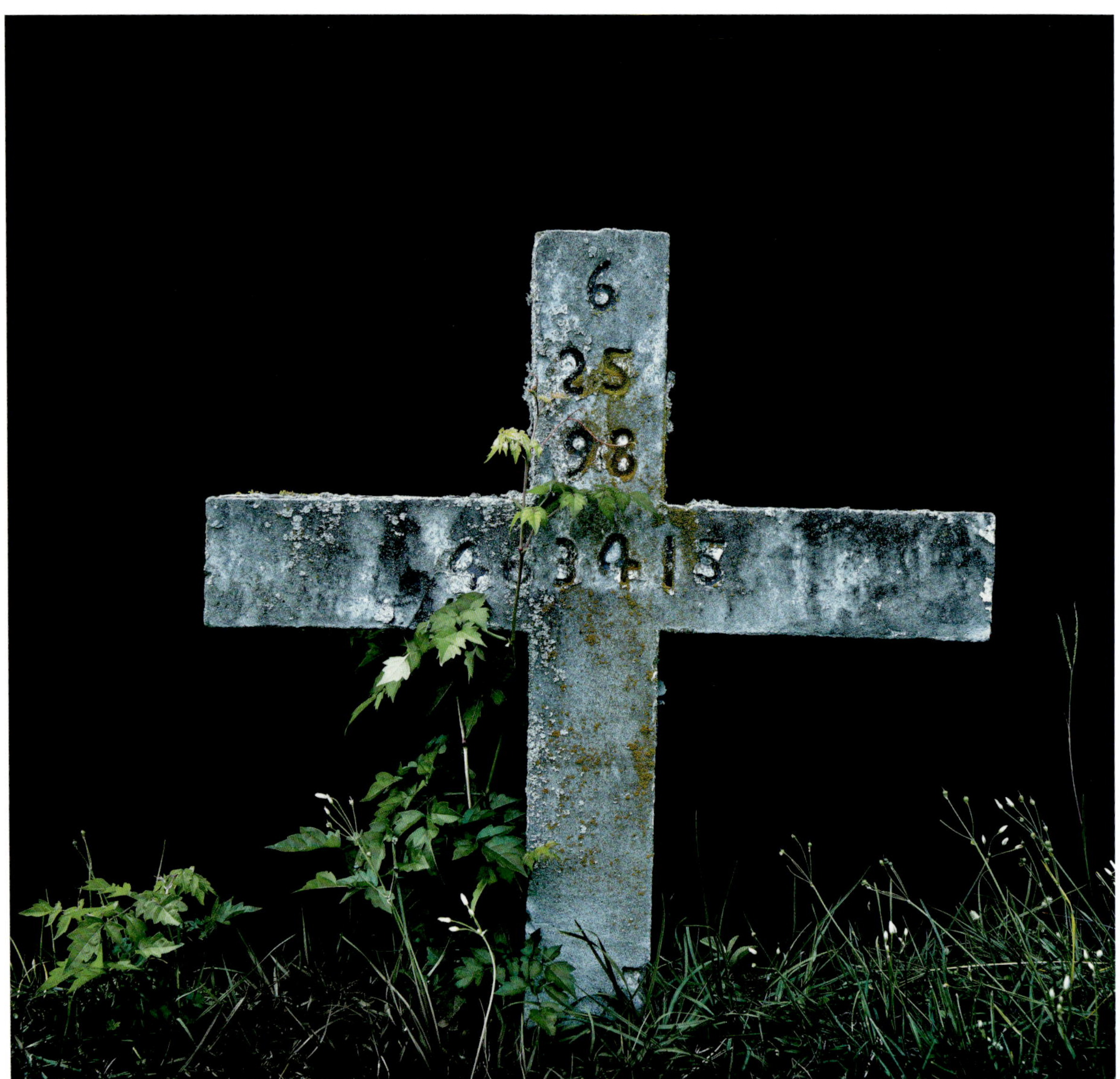

#133

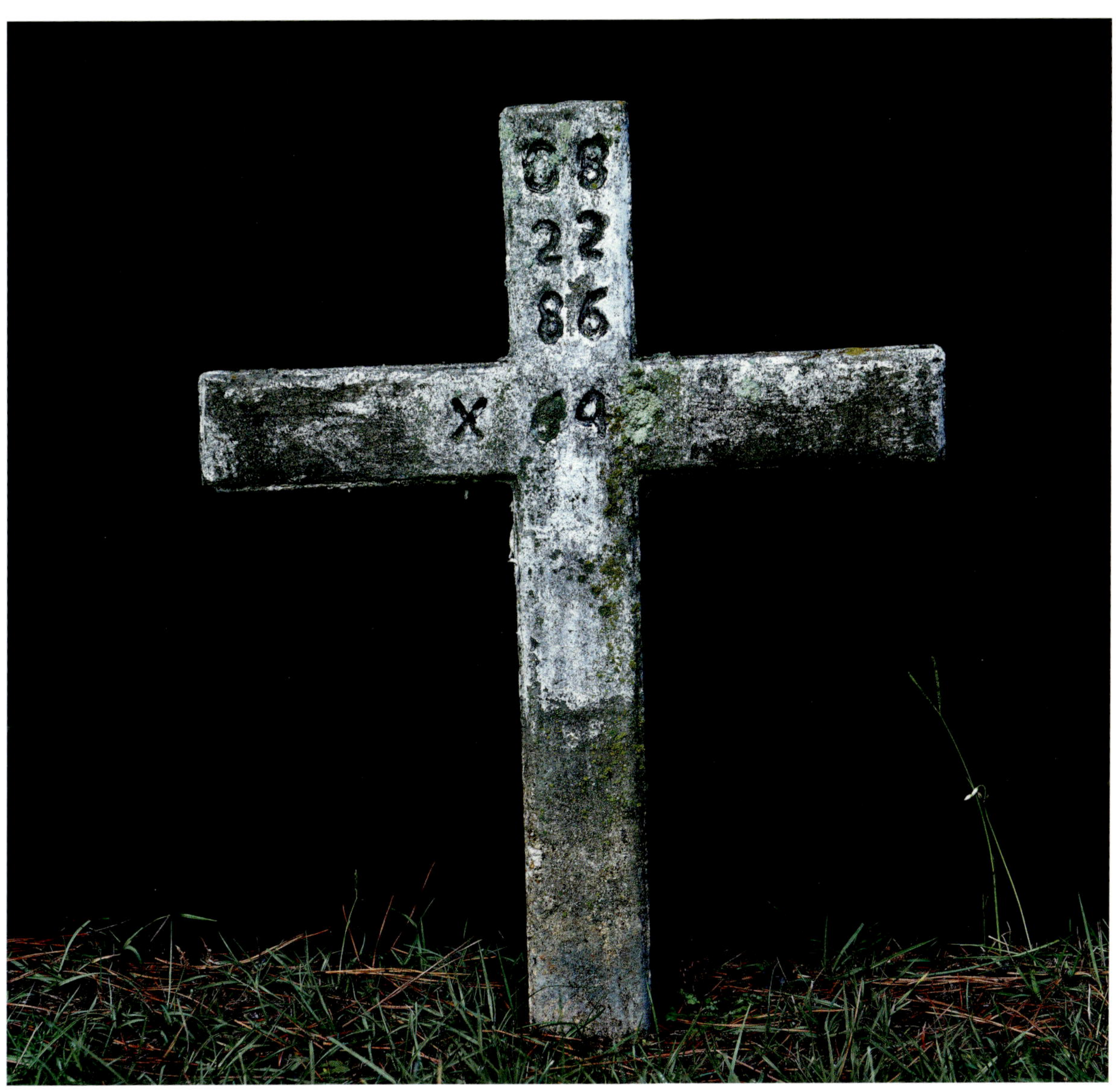

#021

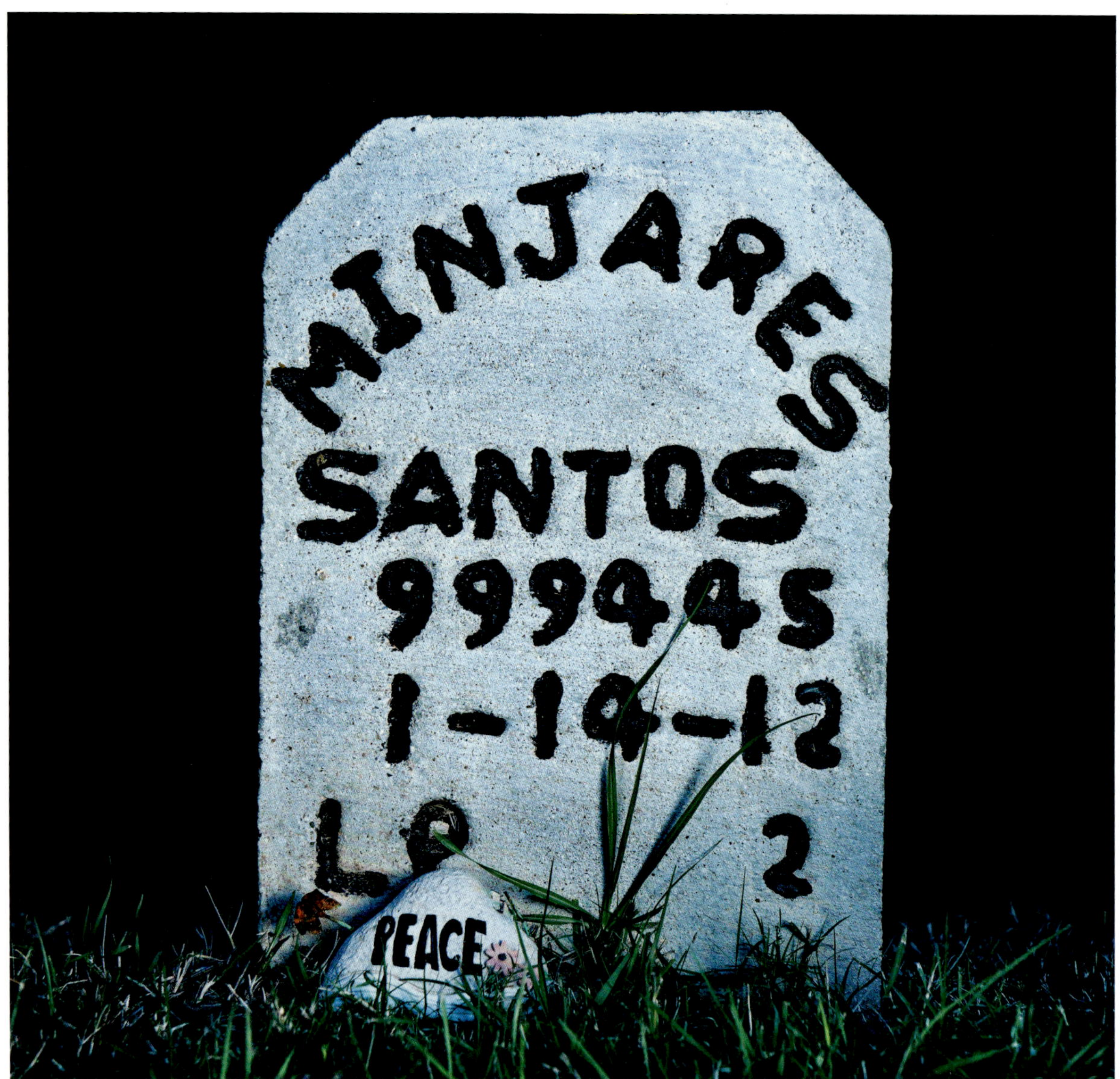

MINJARES
SANTOS
99944S
1-14-12
PEACE

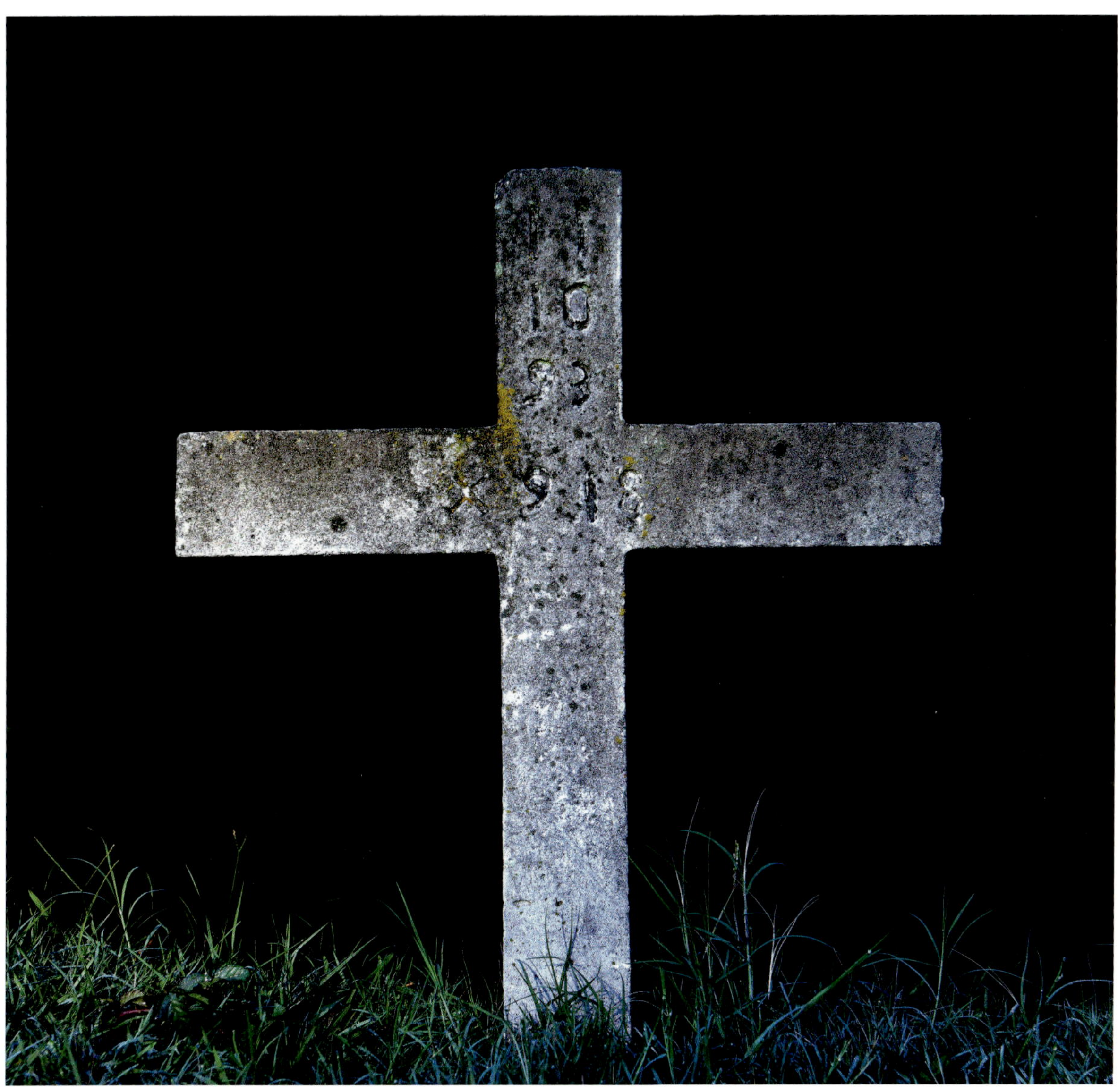

#017

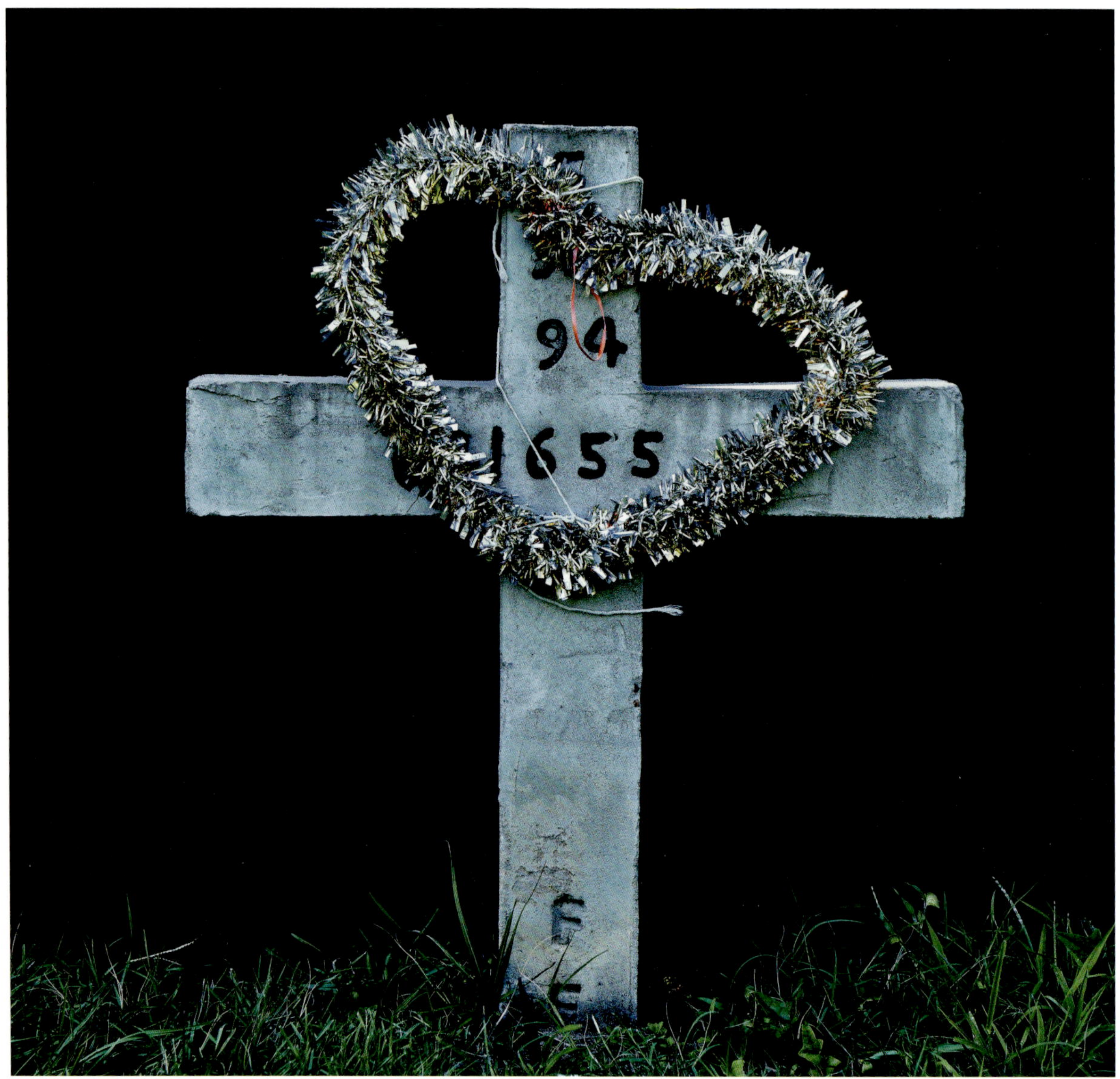

#158

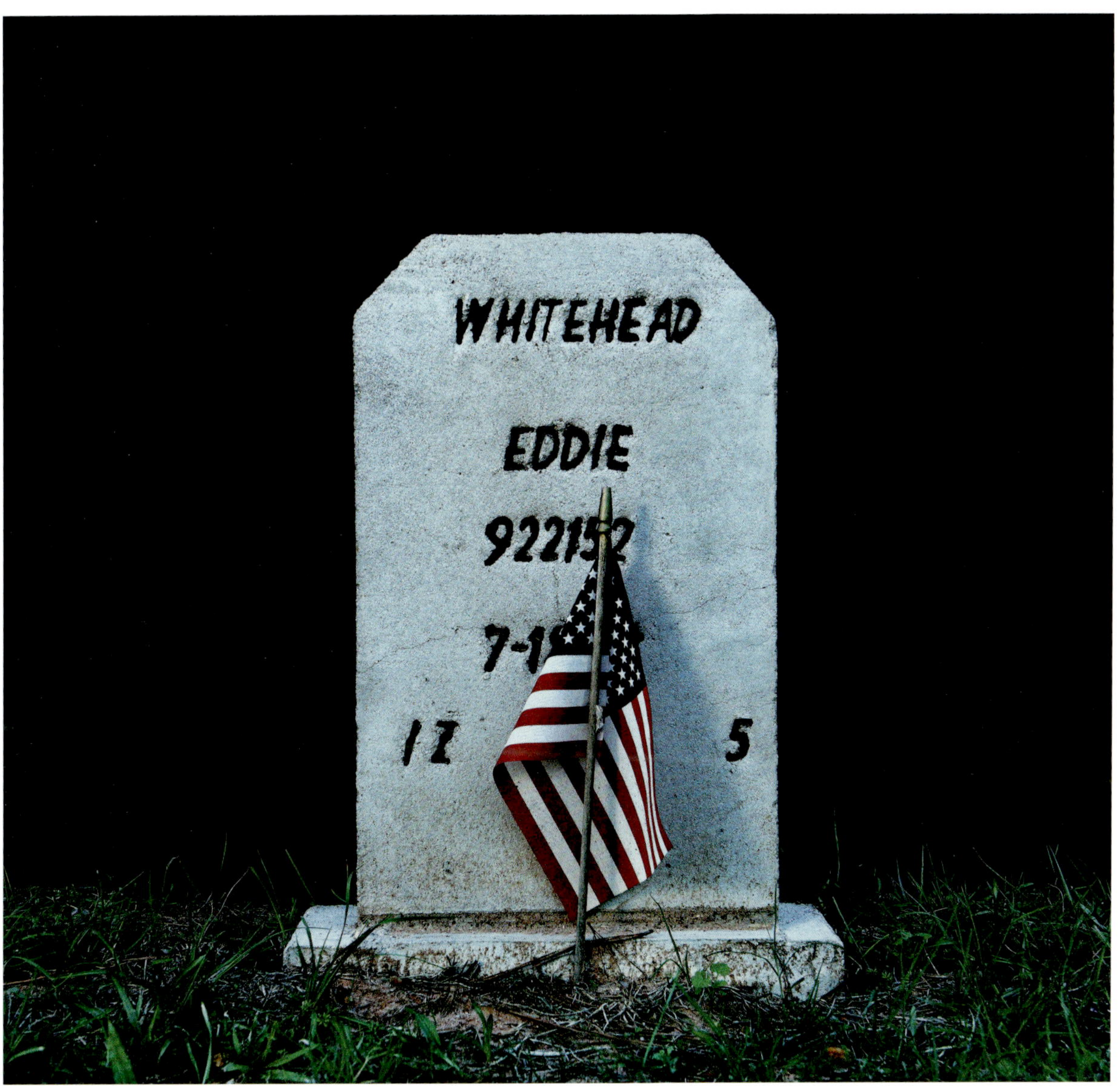

WHITEHEAD
EDDIE
922152
7-1
11
5

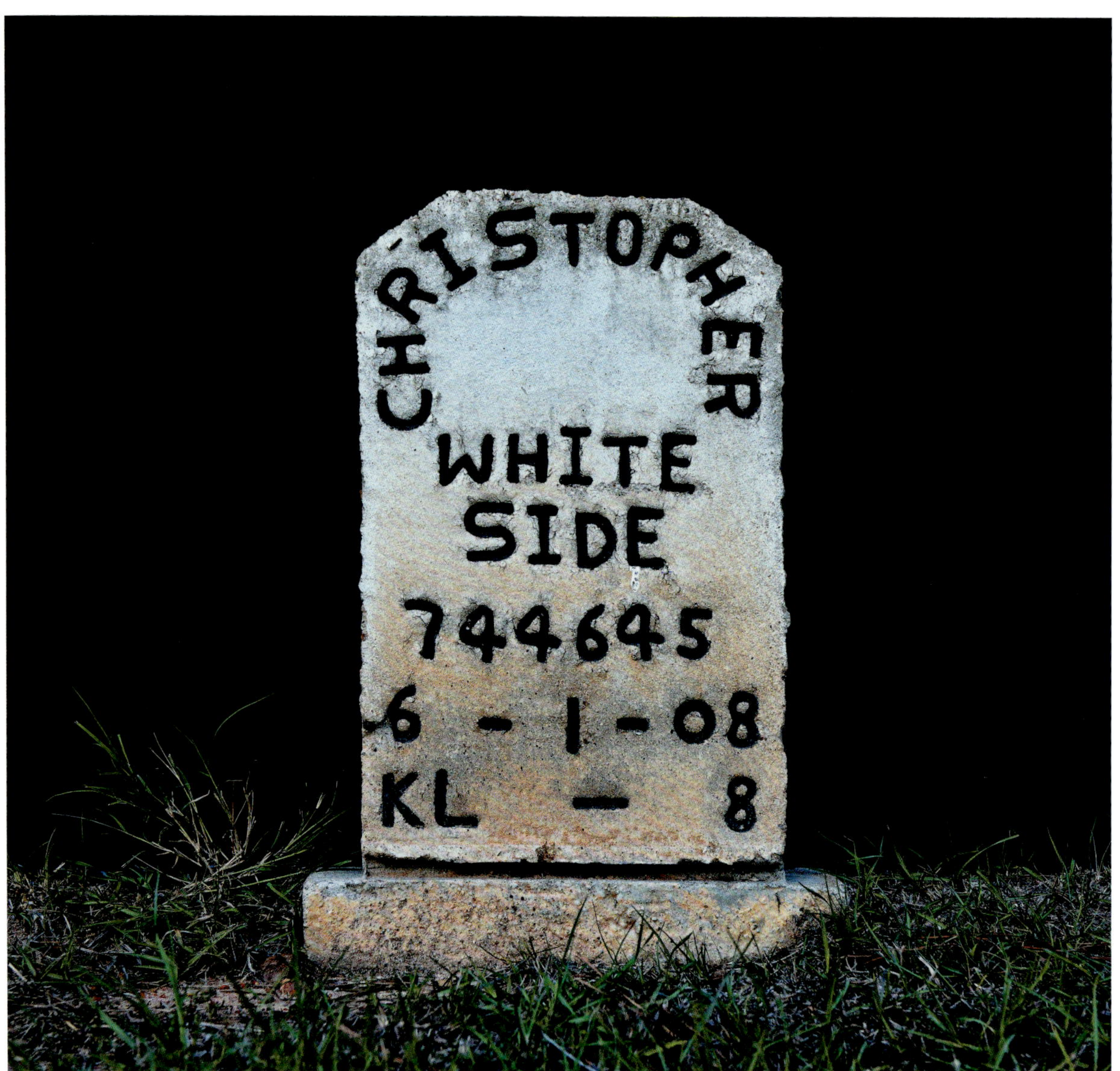

CHRISTOPHER
WHITE
SIDE
744645
6 - 1 - 08
KL — 8

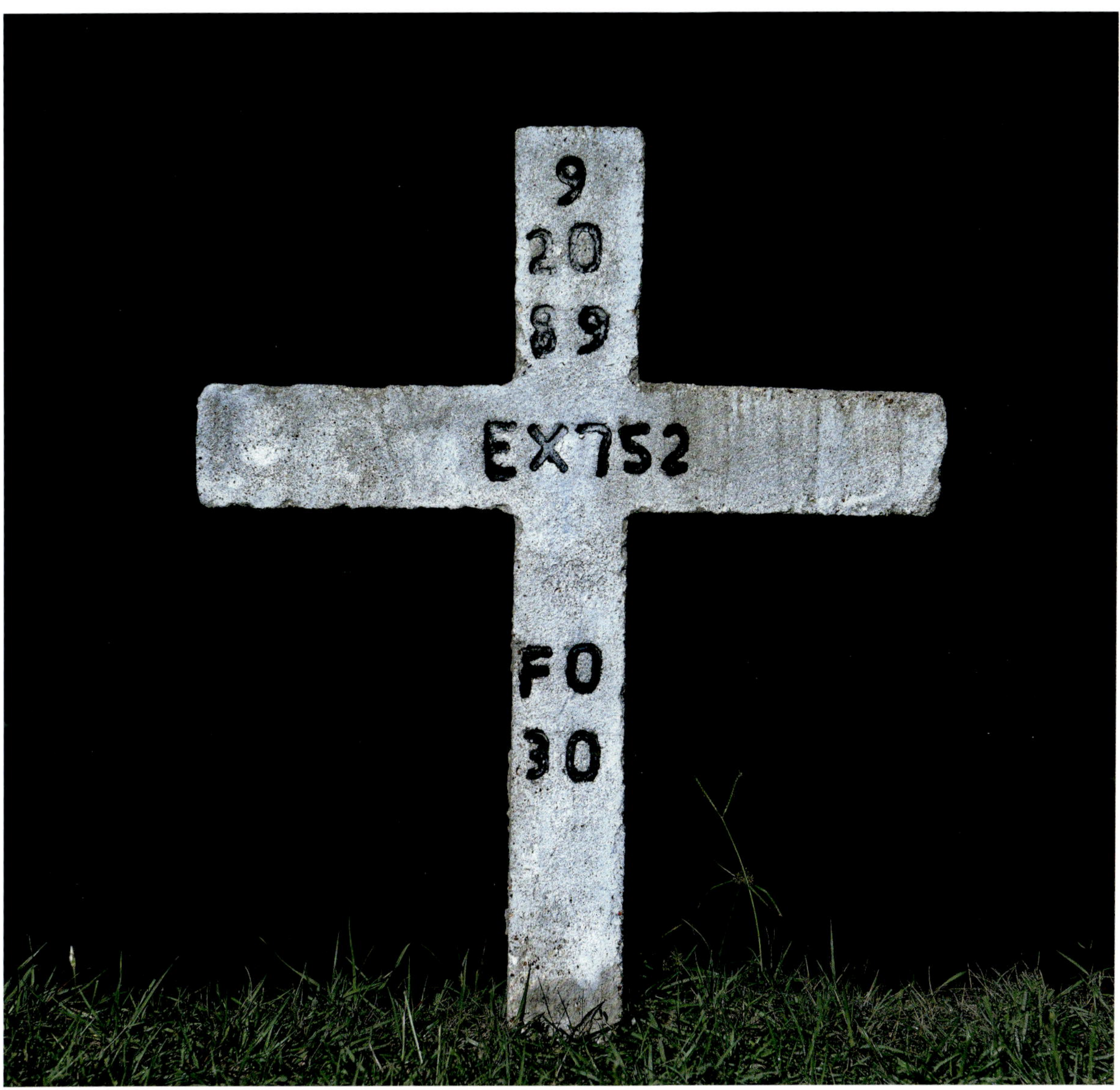

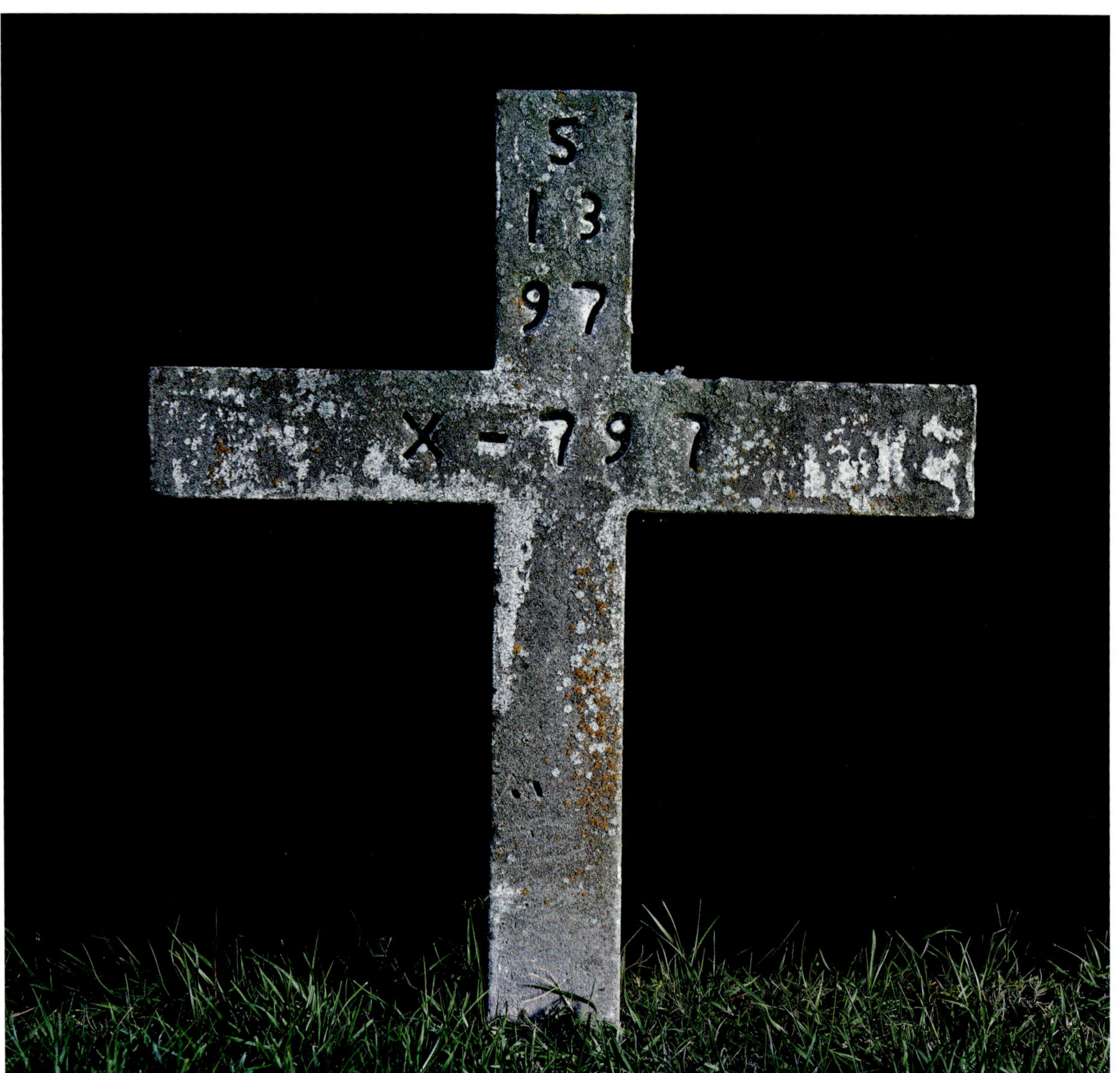

#112

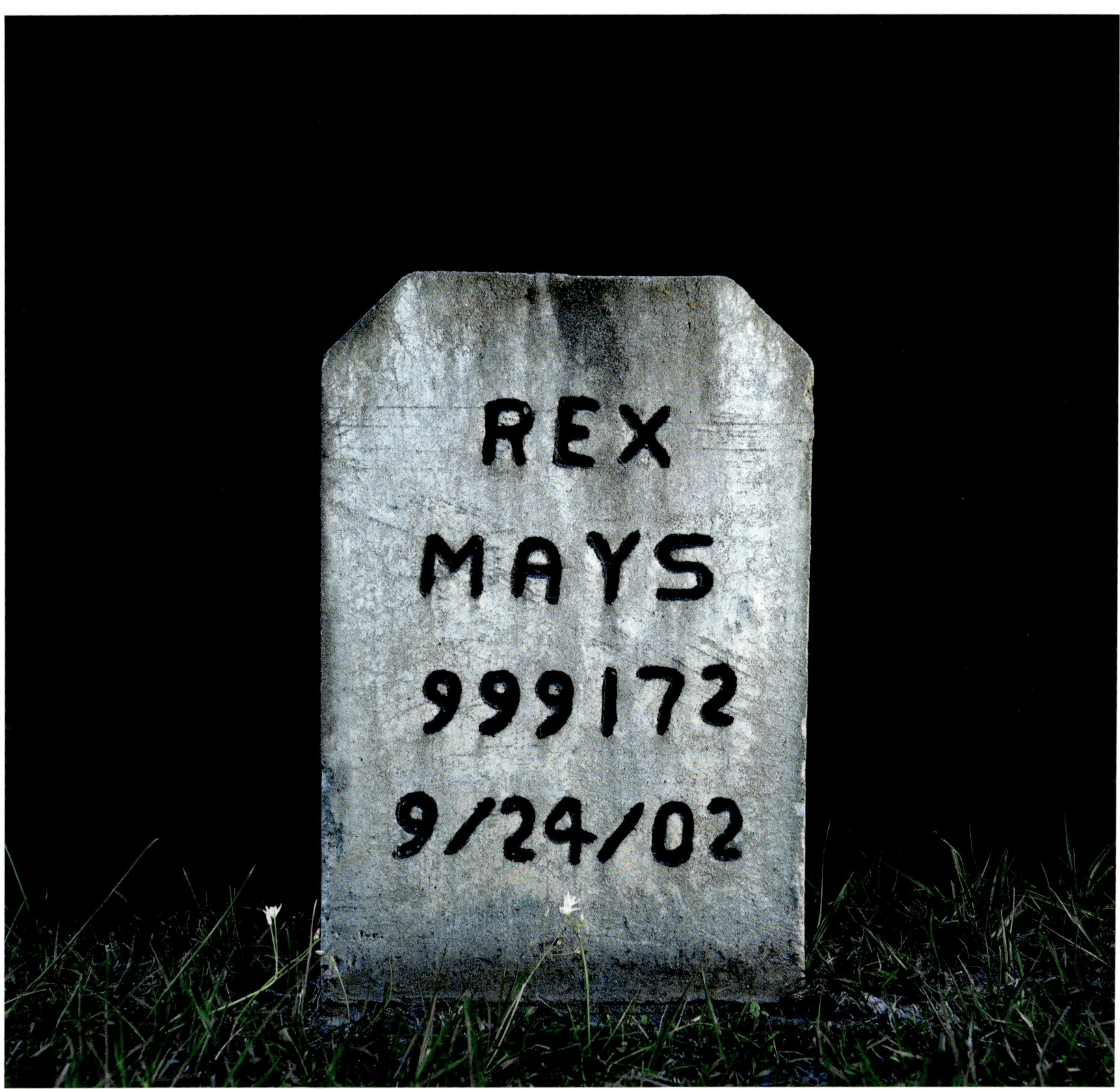

#071

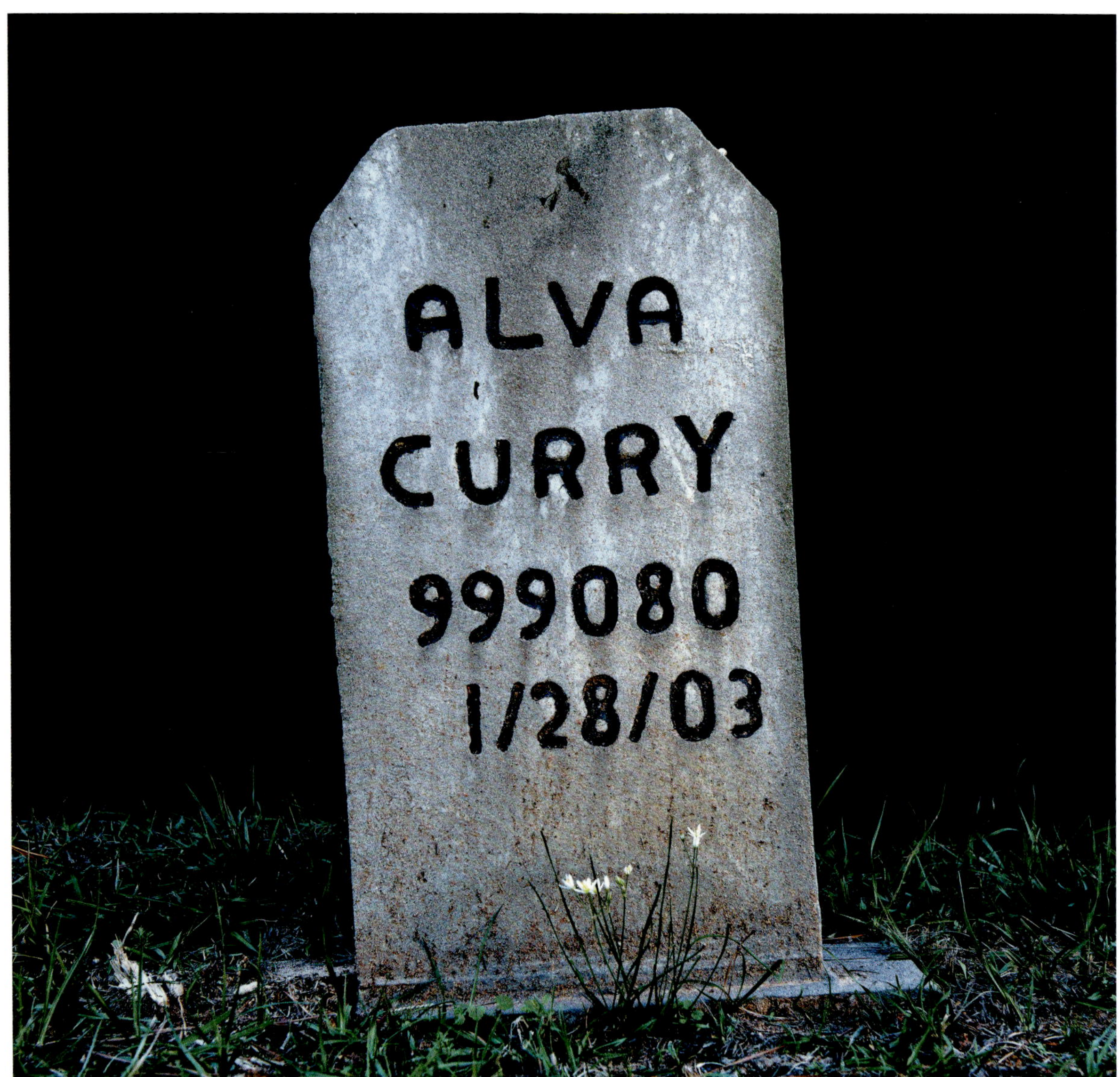

#073

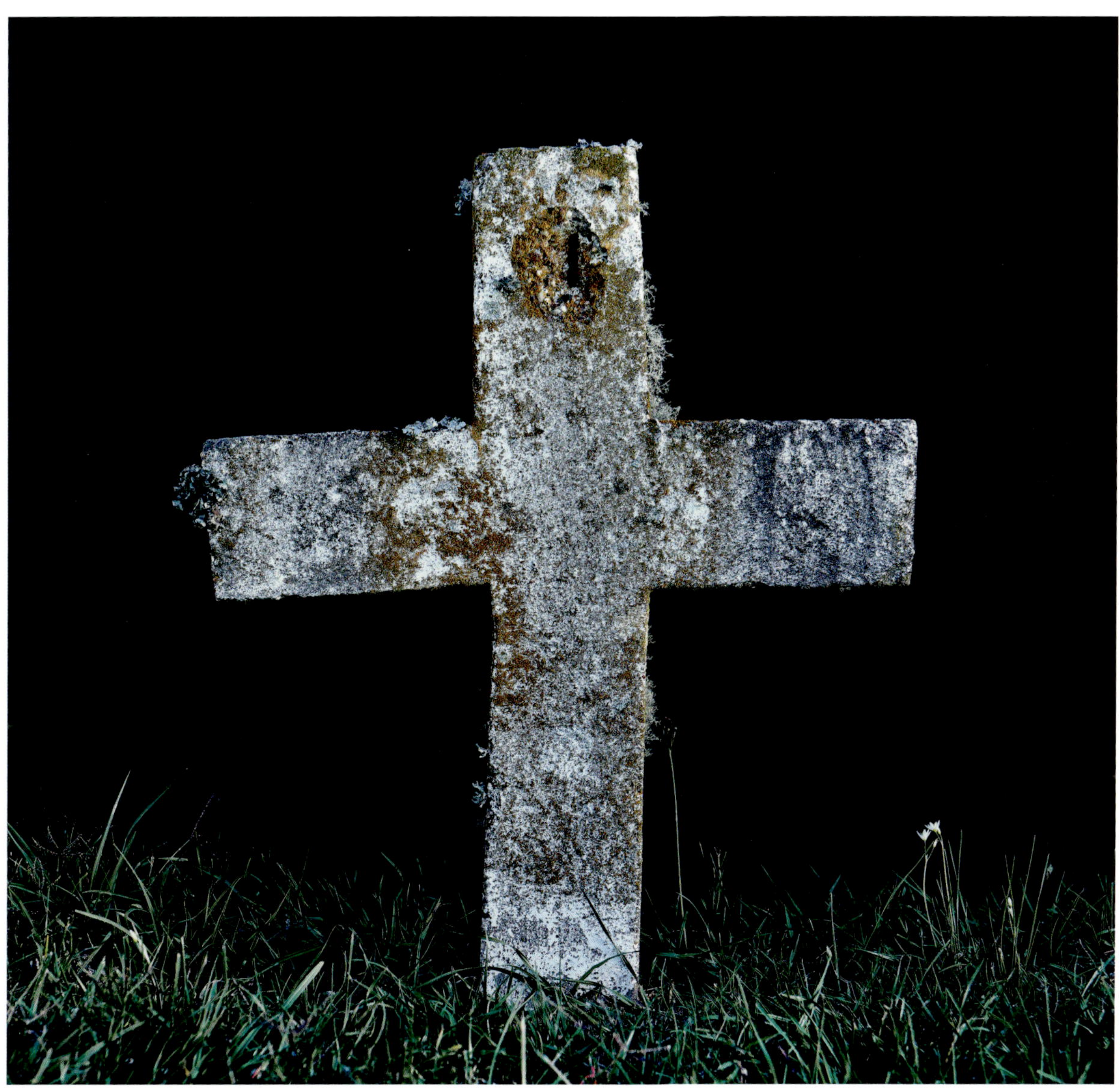

#175

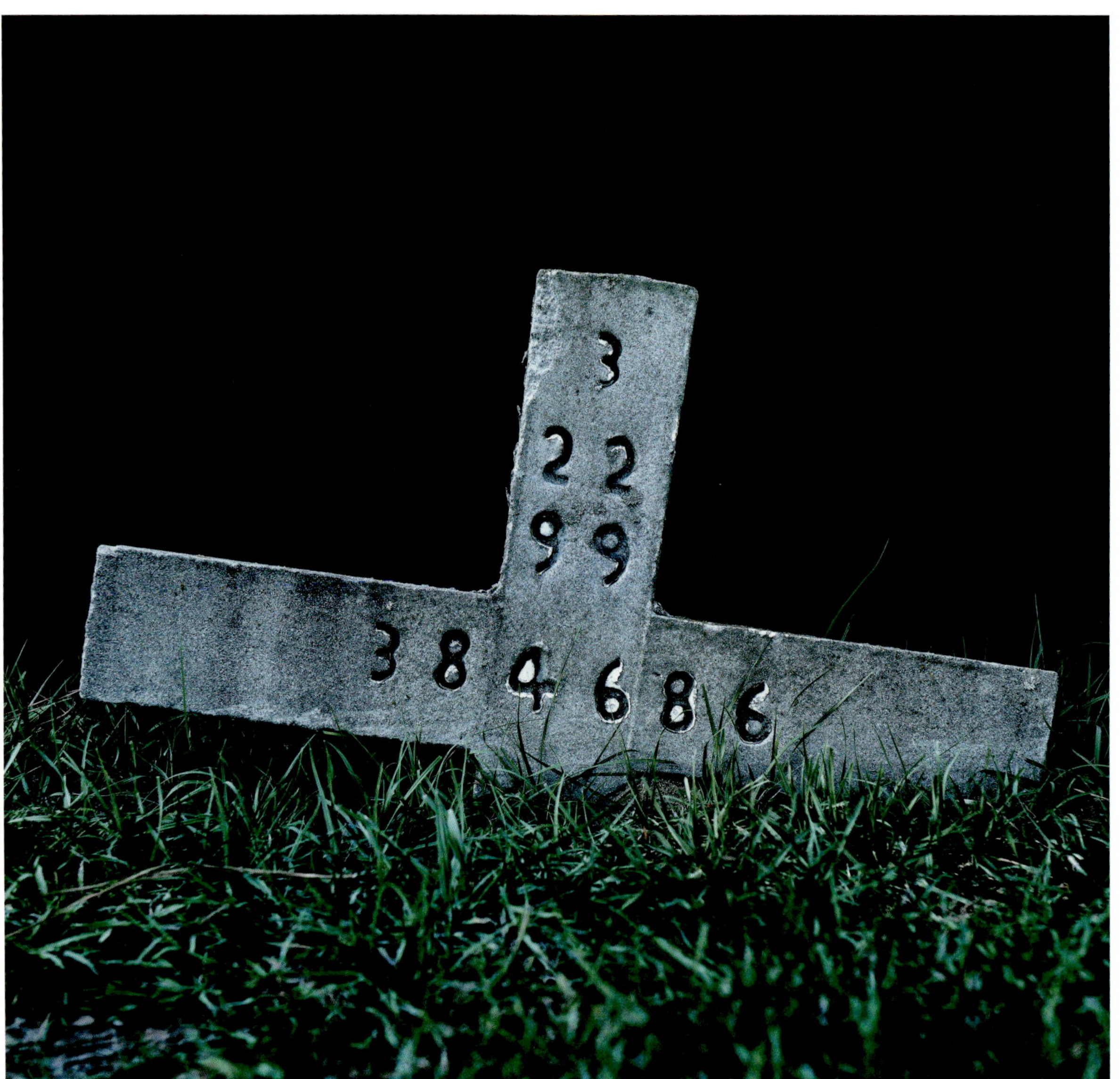

#153

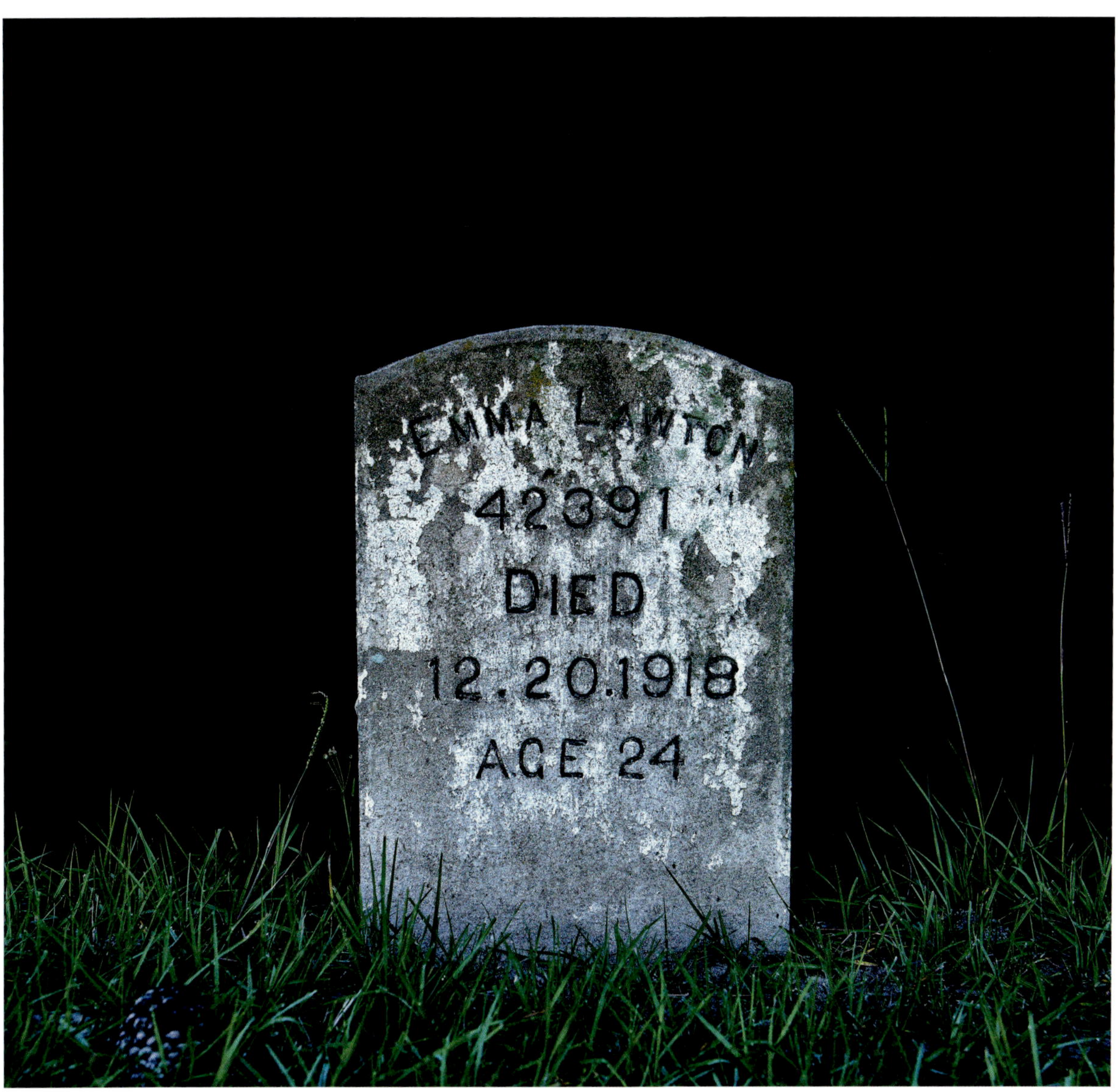

#007

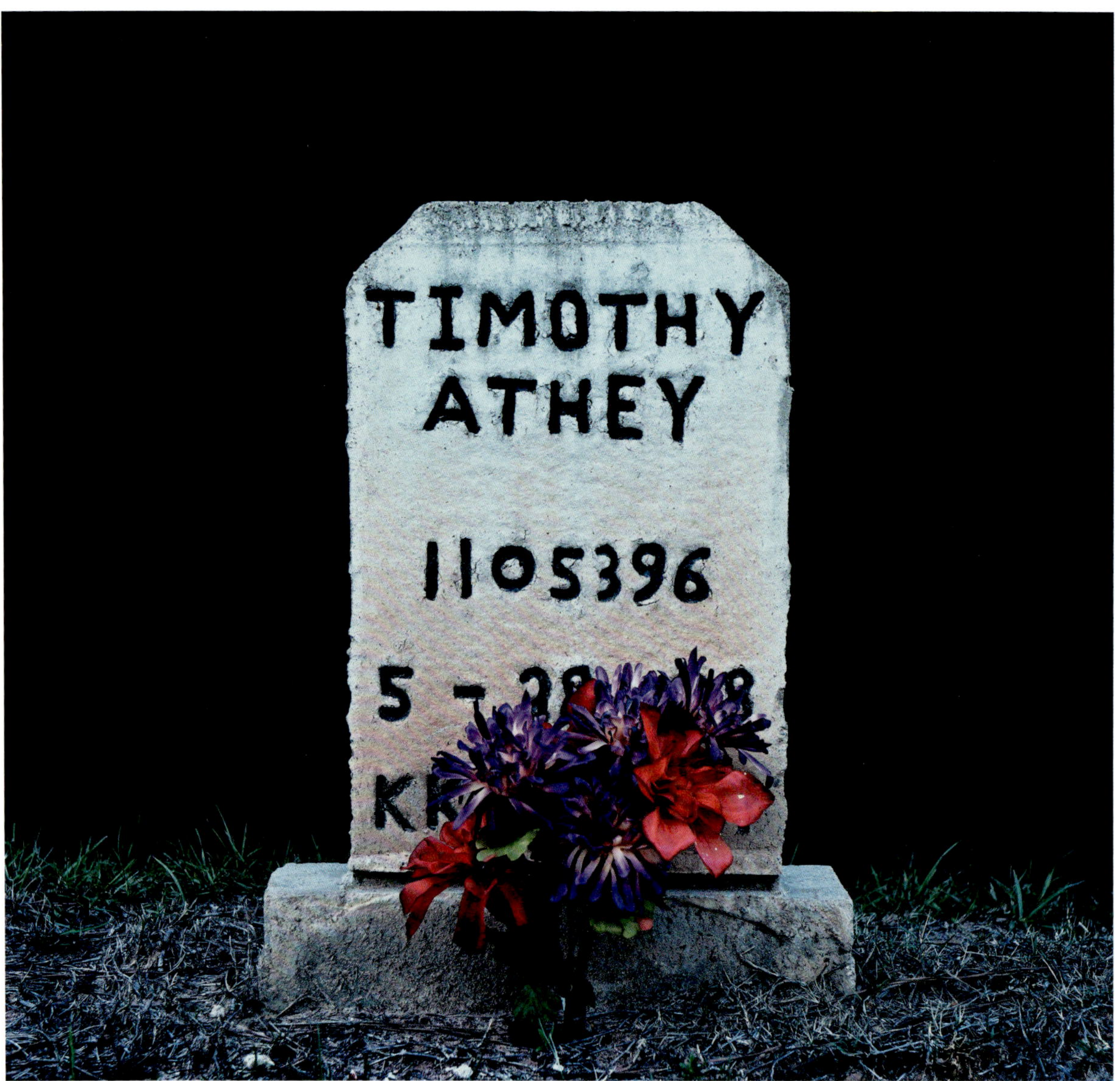

#166

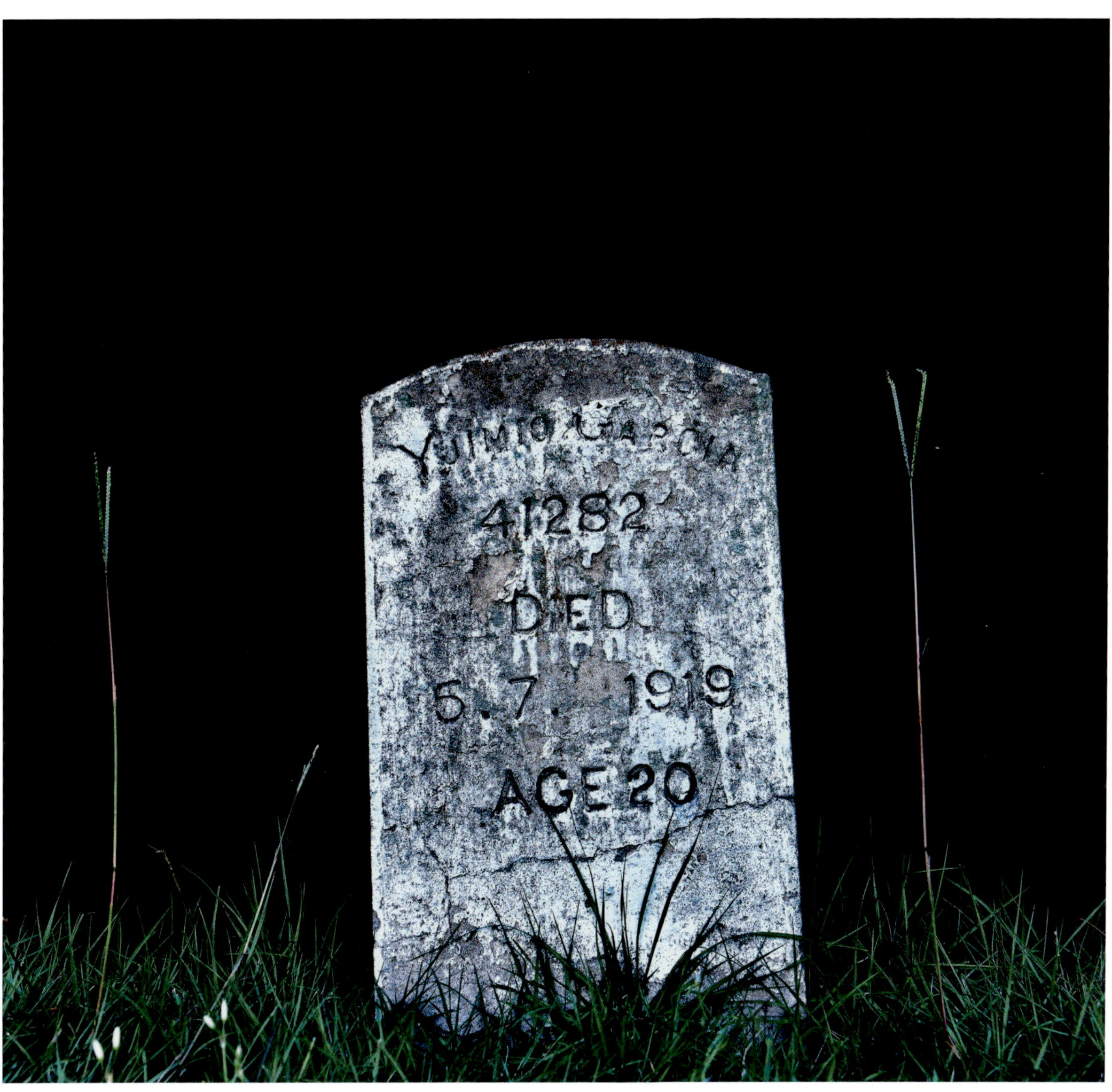

#085

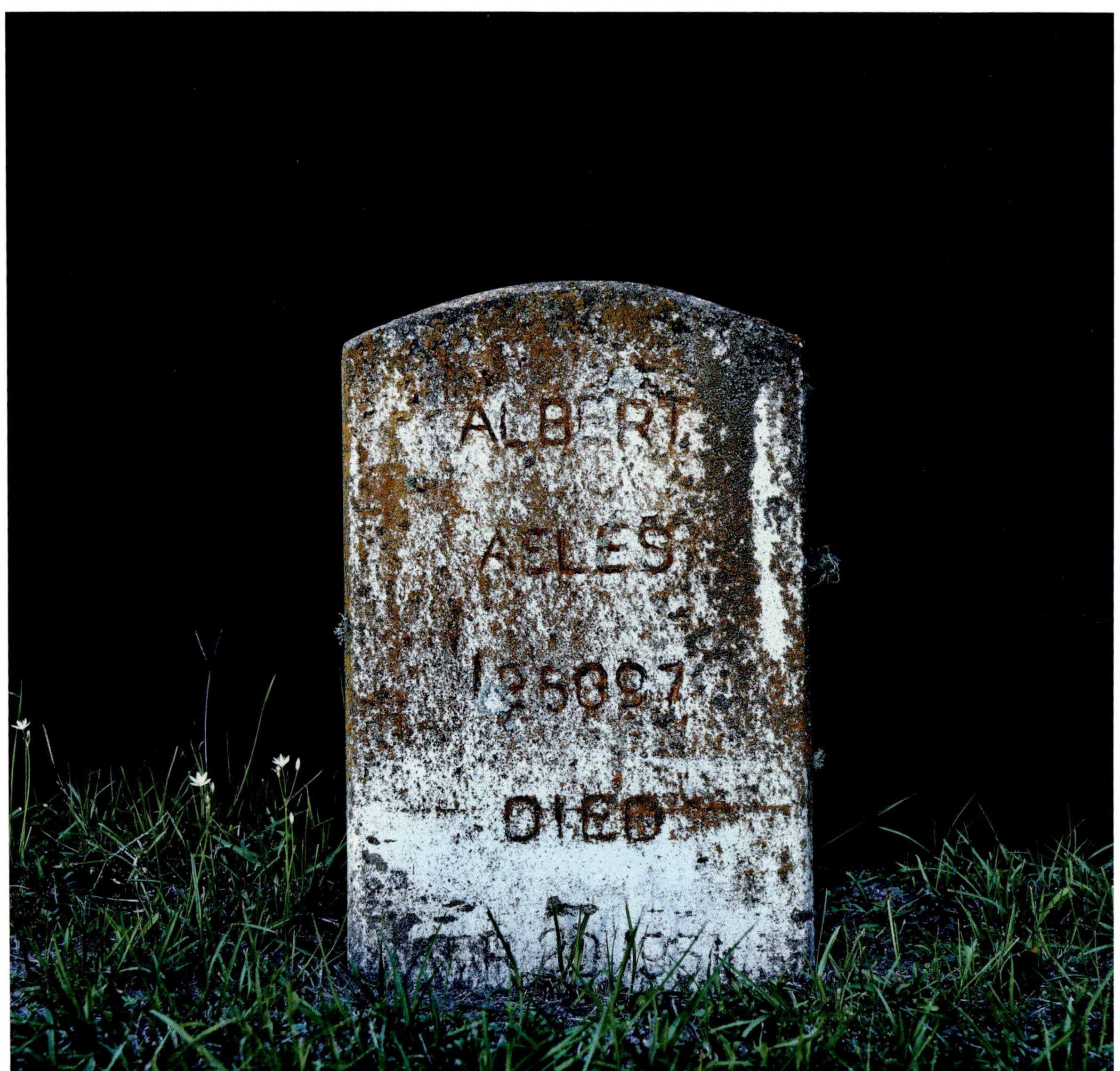

#120

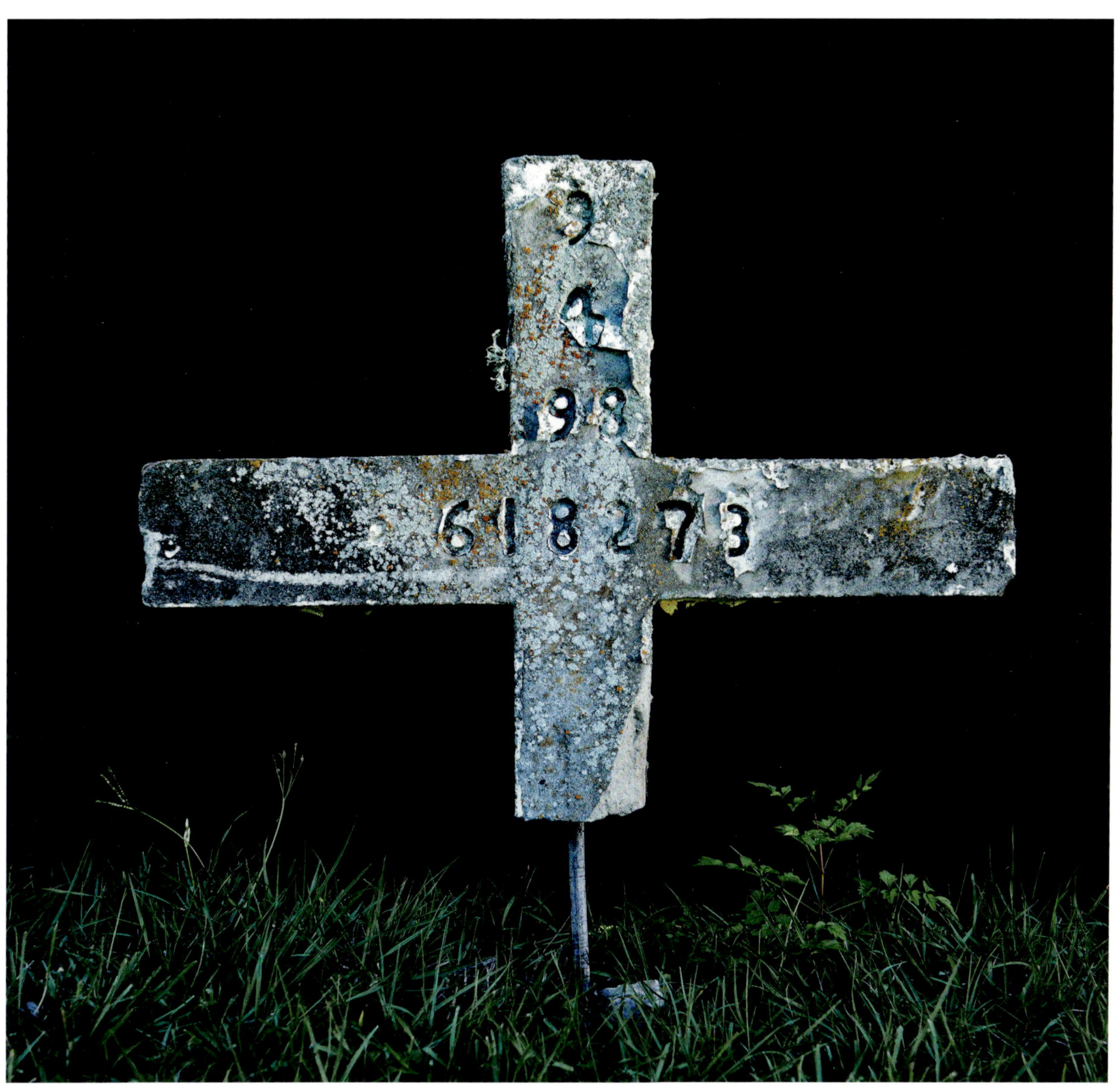

#159

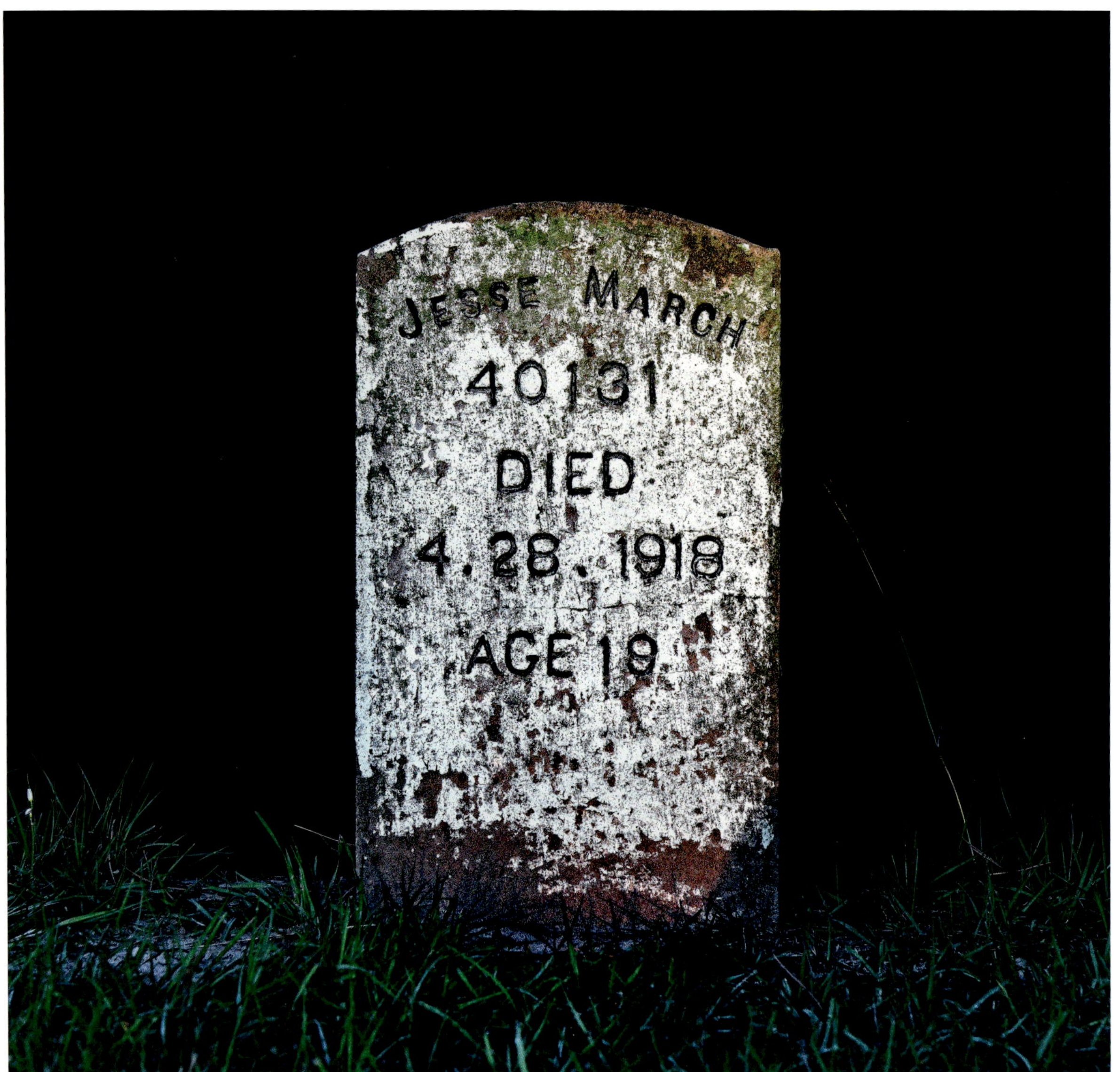

#091

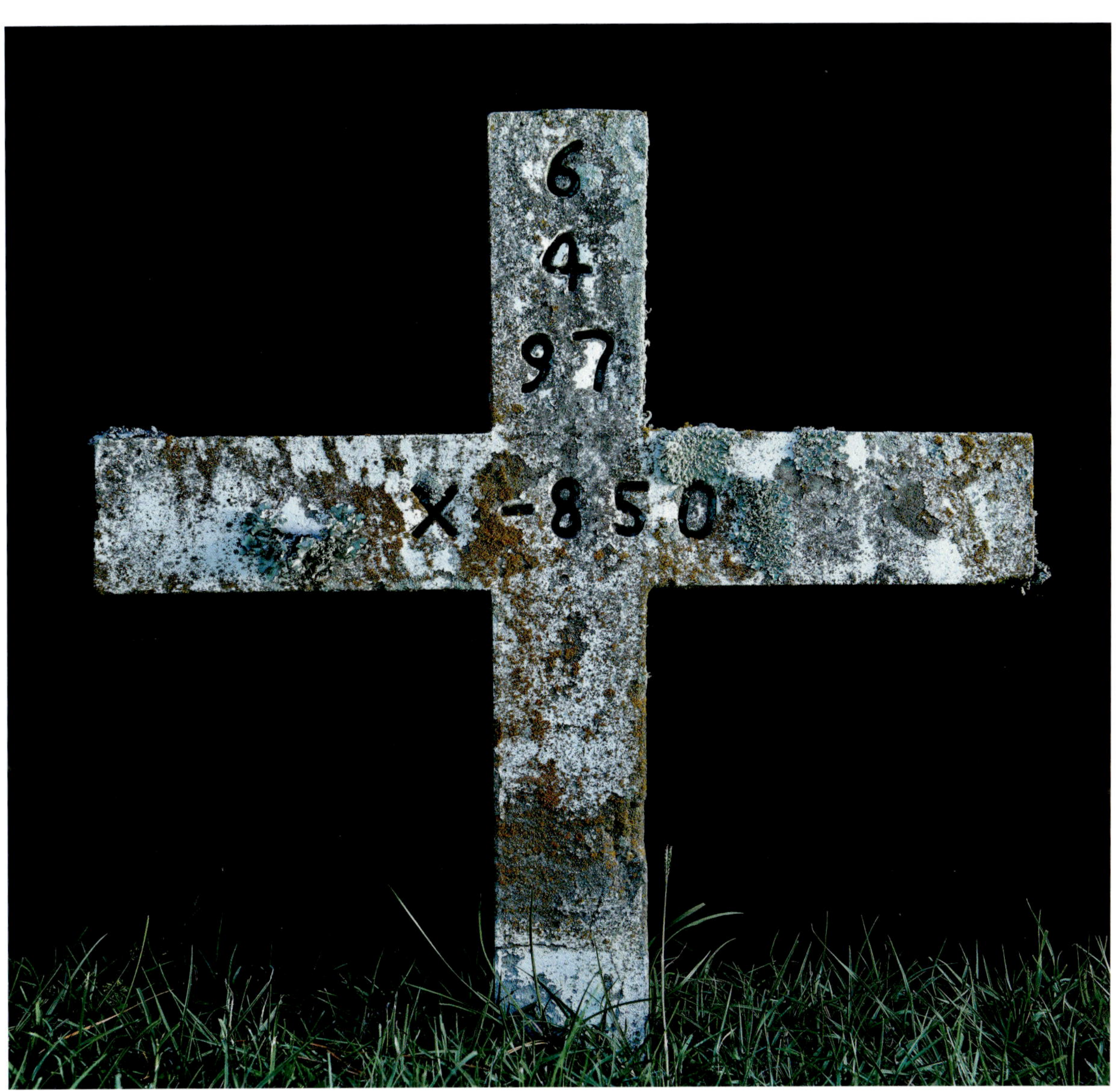

#109

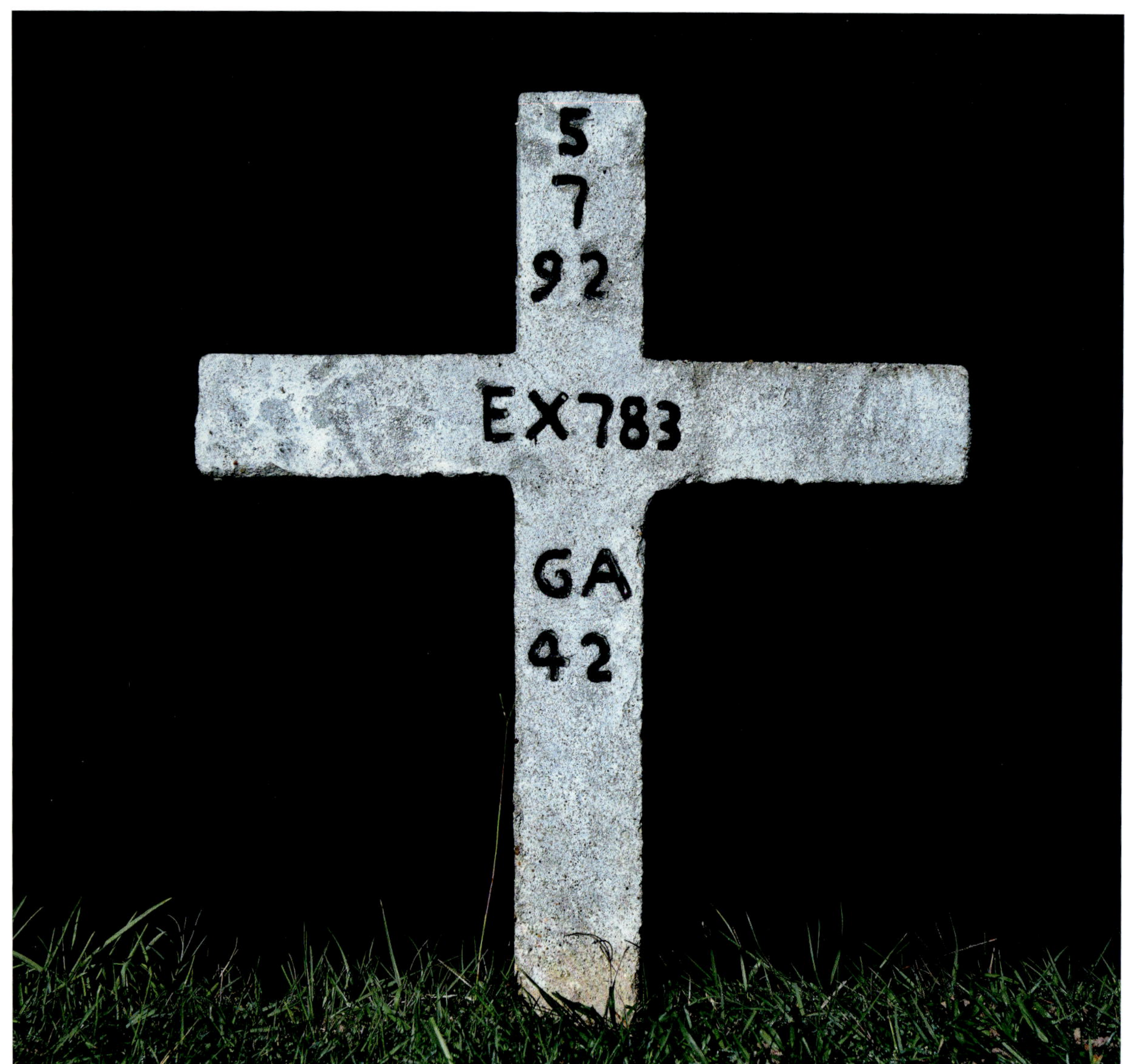

#019

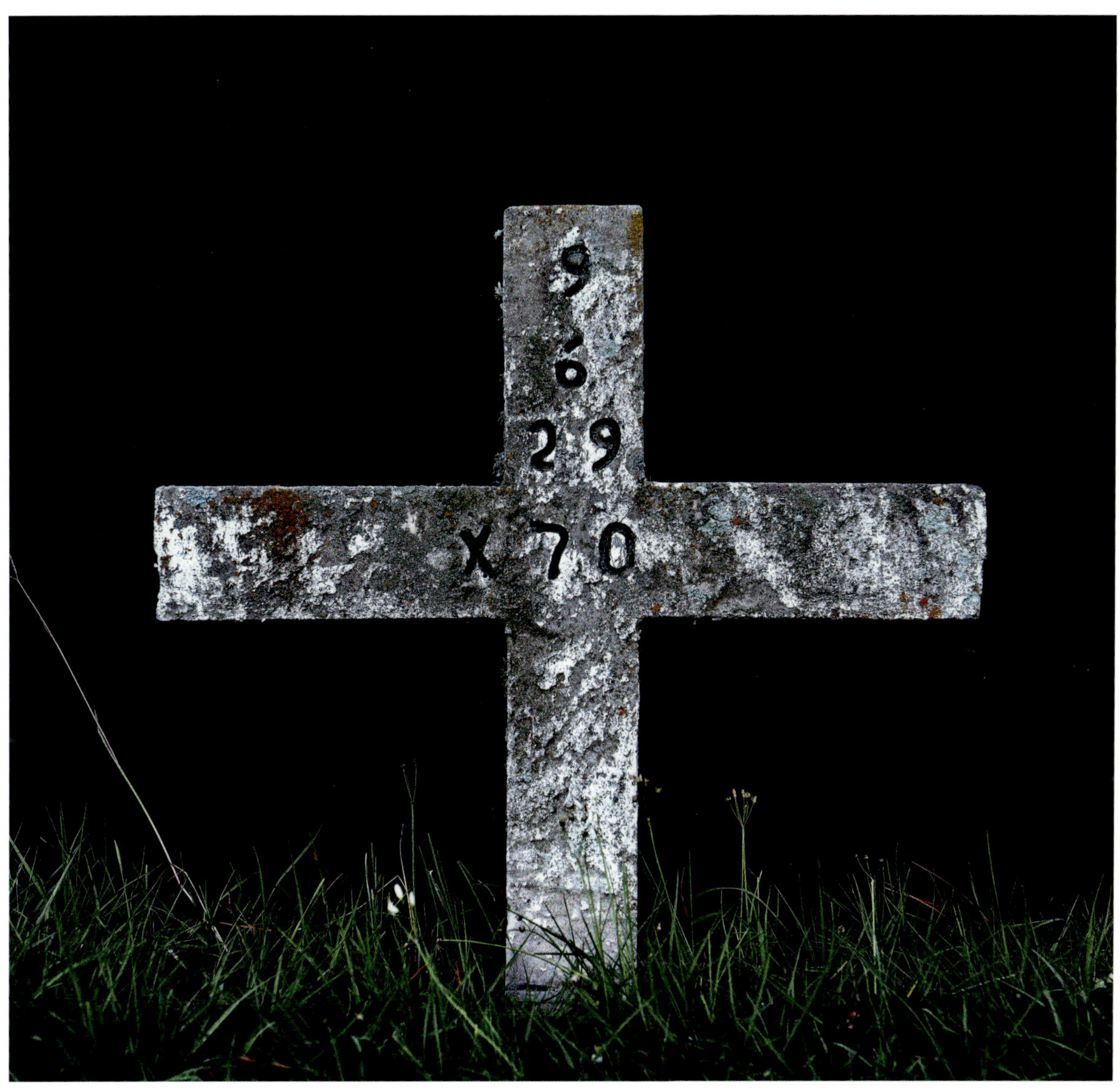

#078

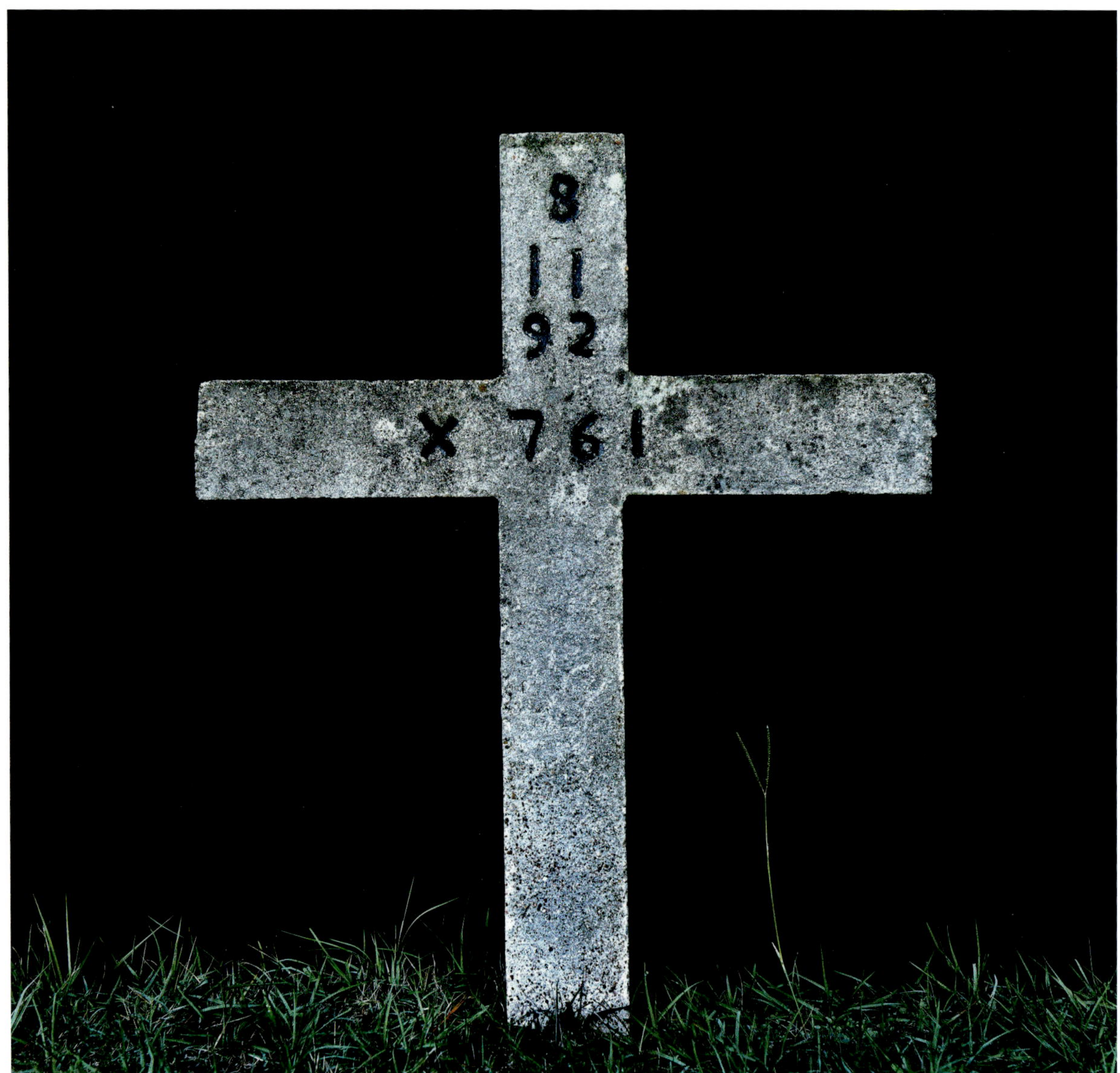

#018

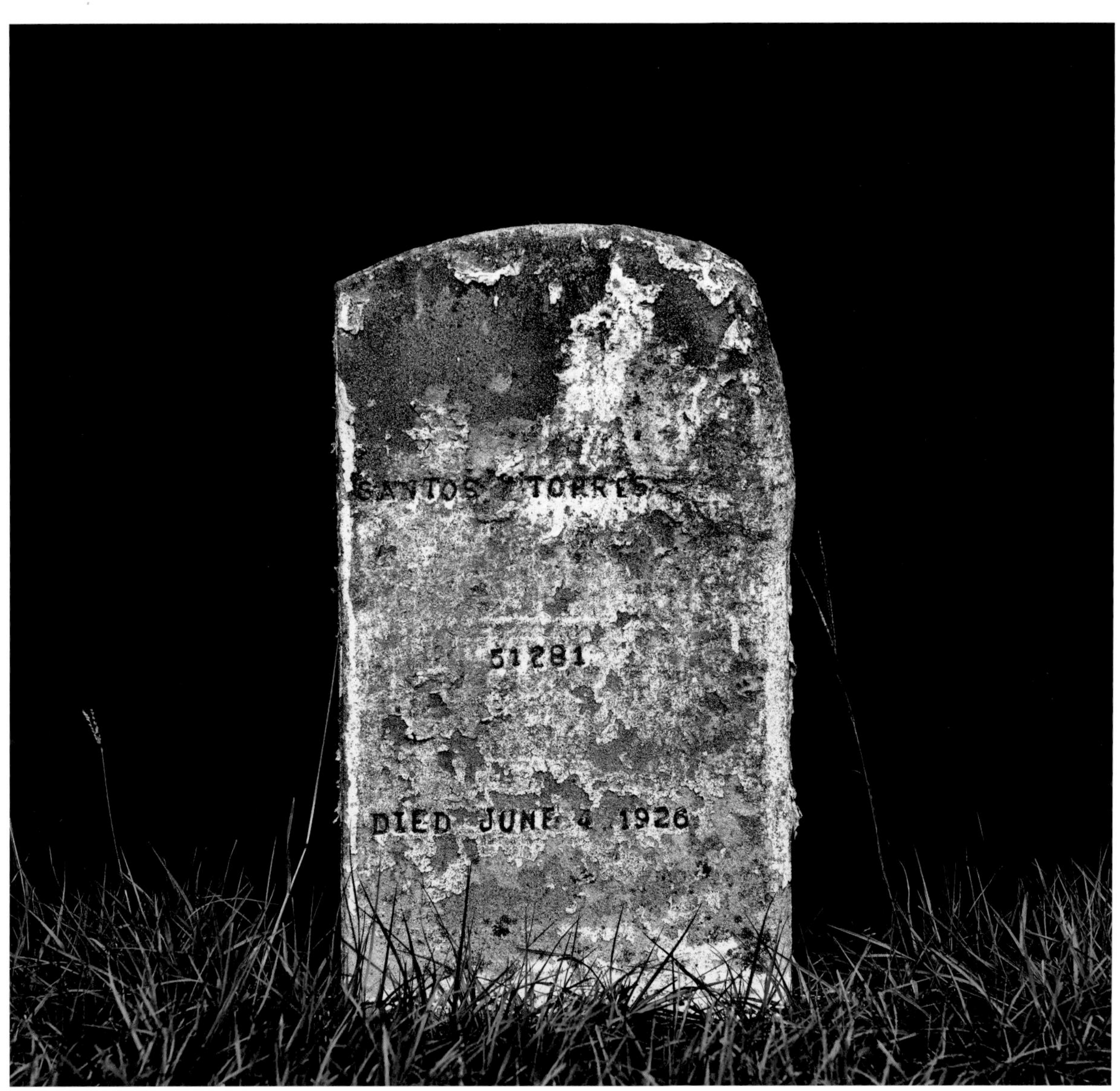

SANTOS TORRES
51281
DIED JUNE 4 1926

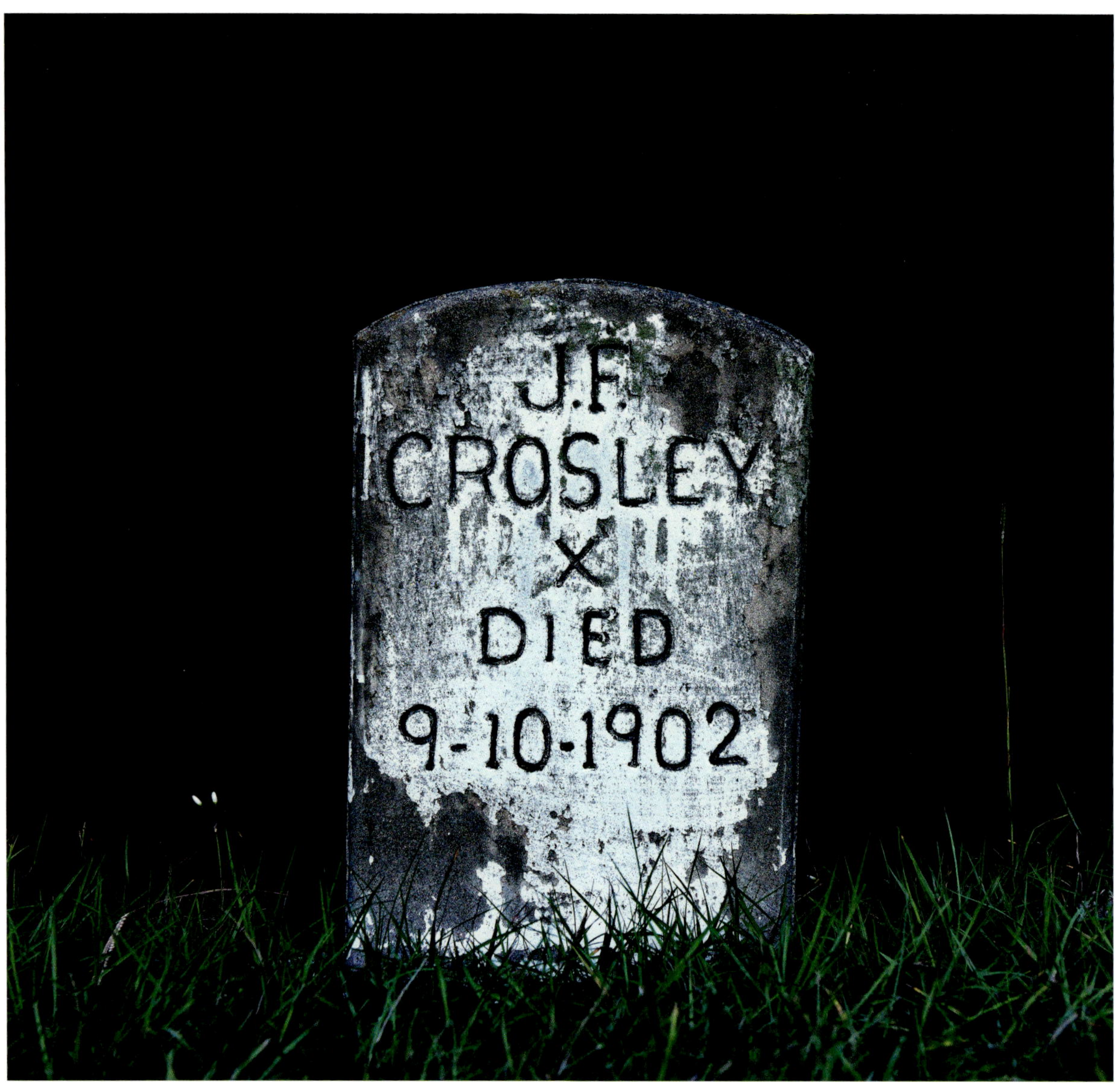

#138

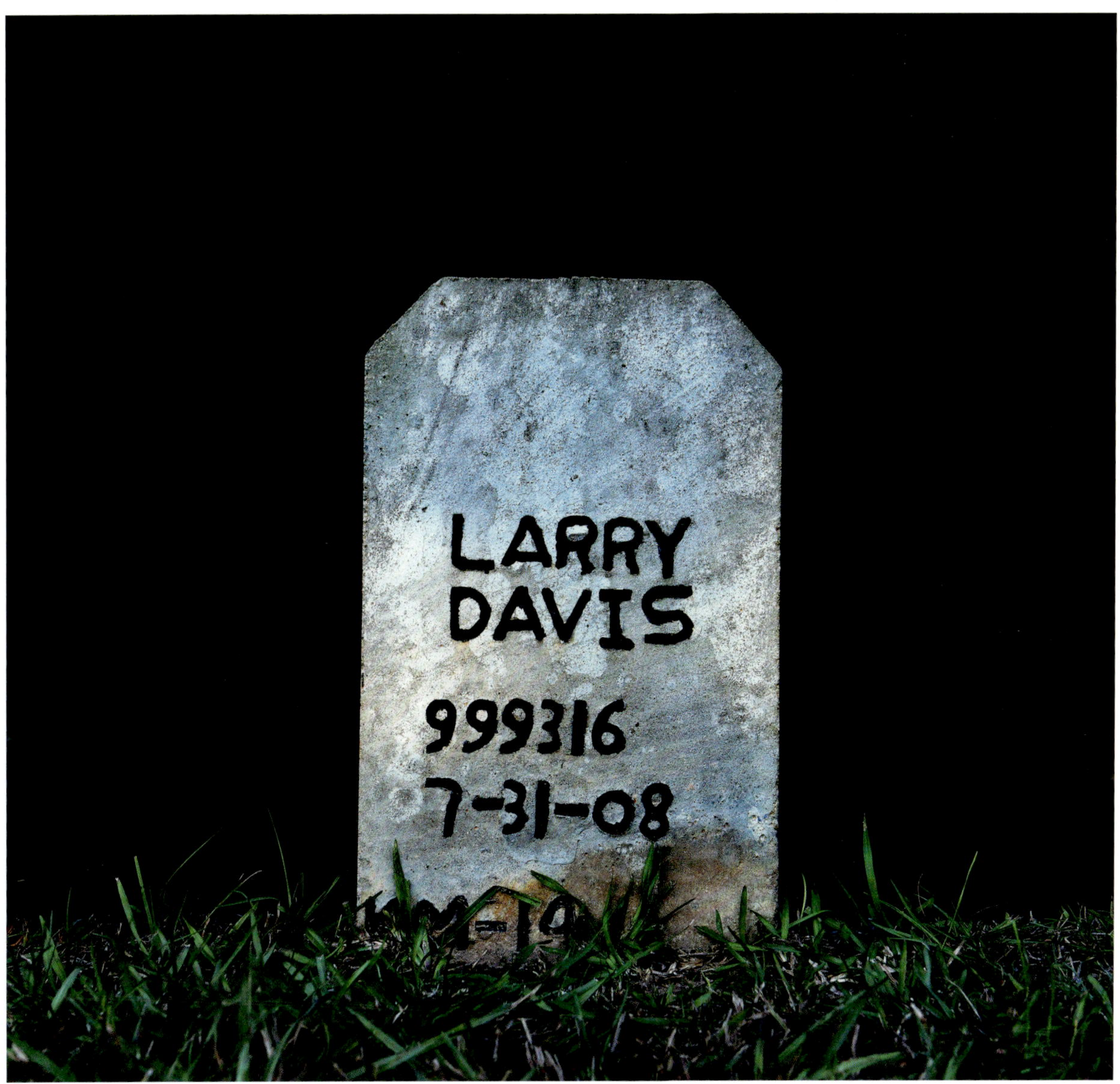

LARRY
DAVIS
999316
7-31-08

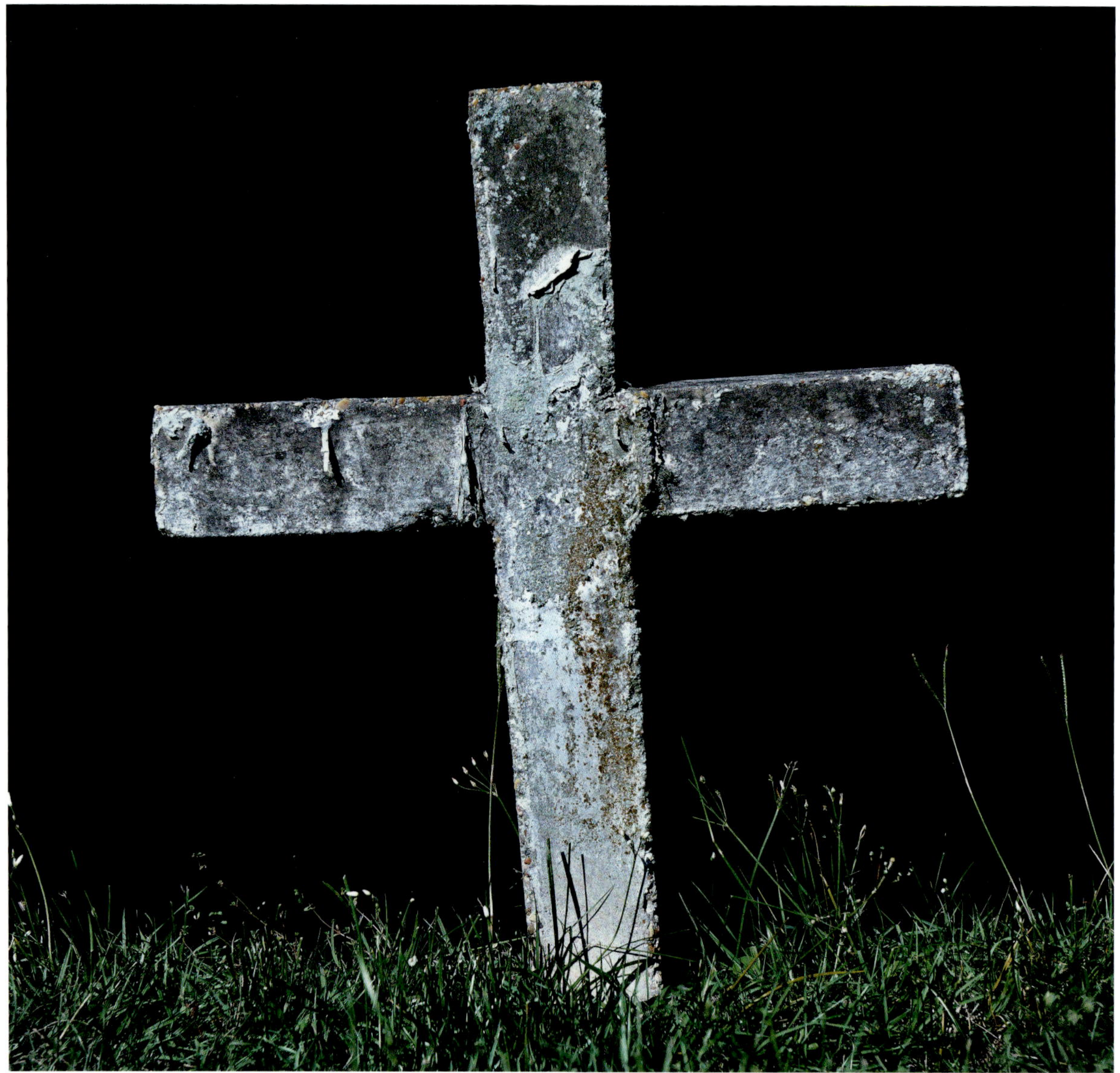

#167

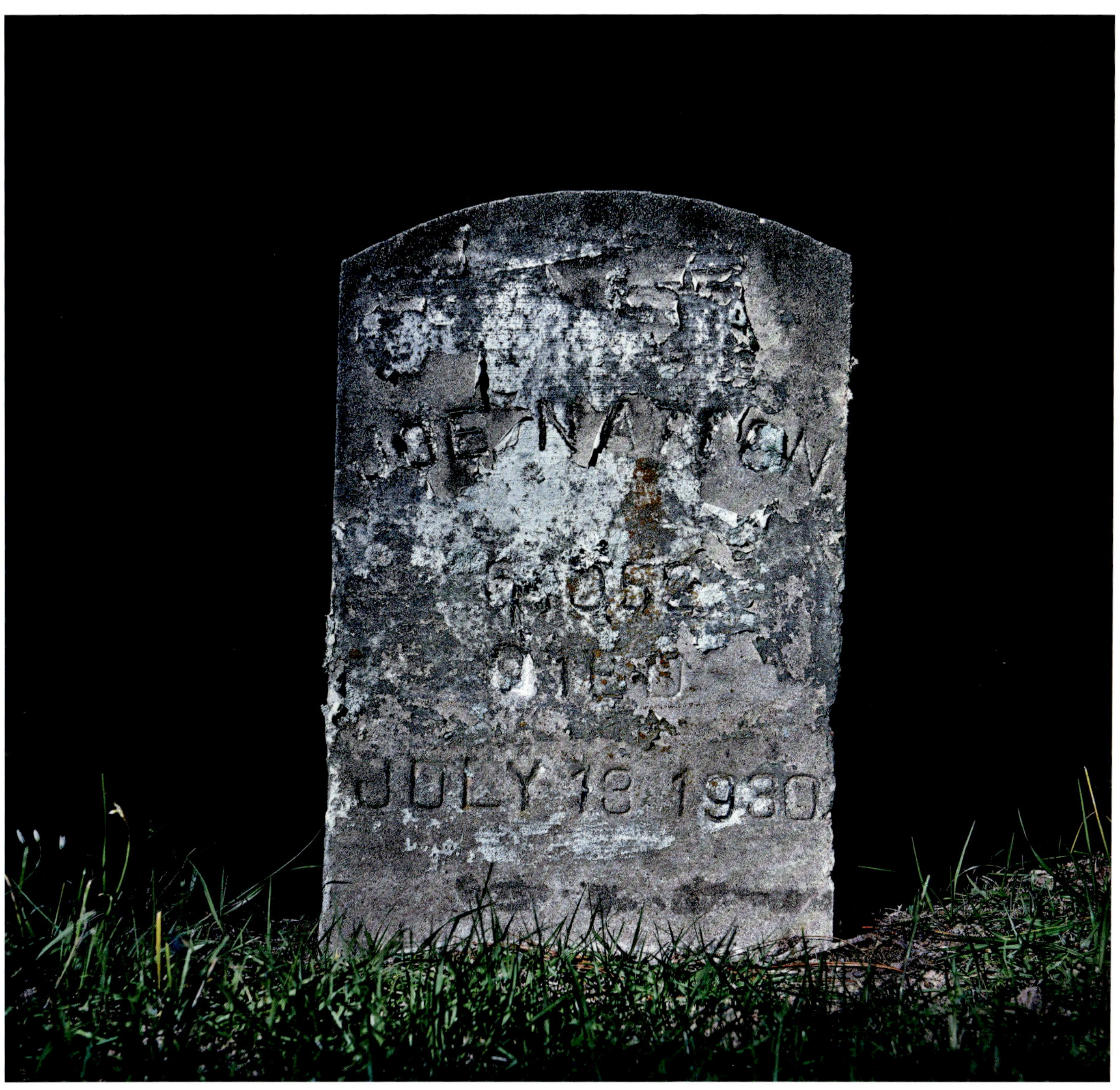
JOE NATION
ROSE
DIED
JULY 18 1980

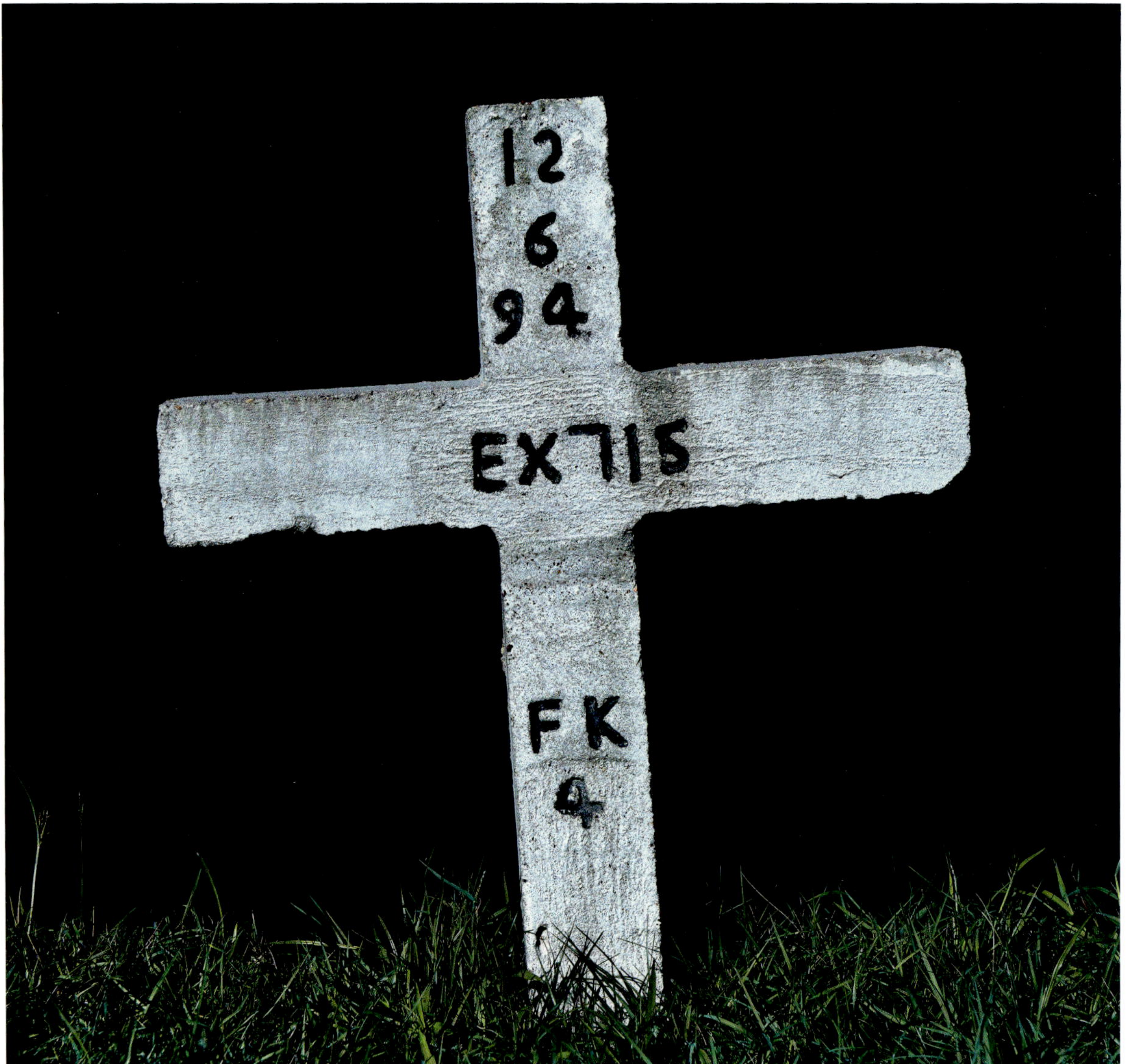

12
6
94
EX715
FK
4

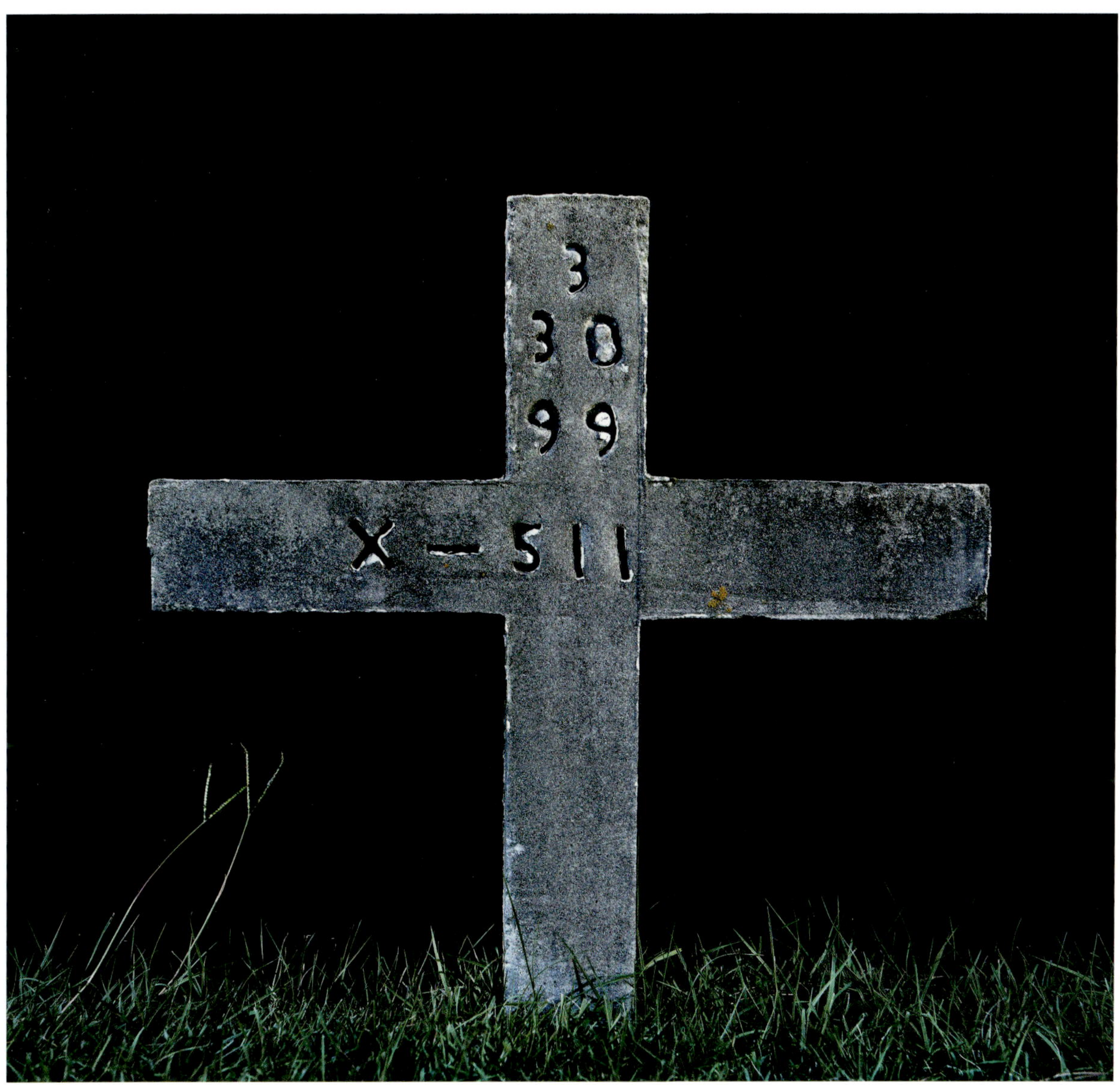

#108

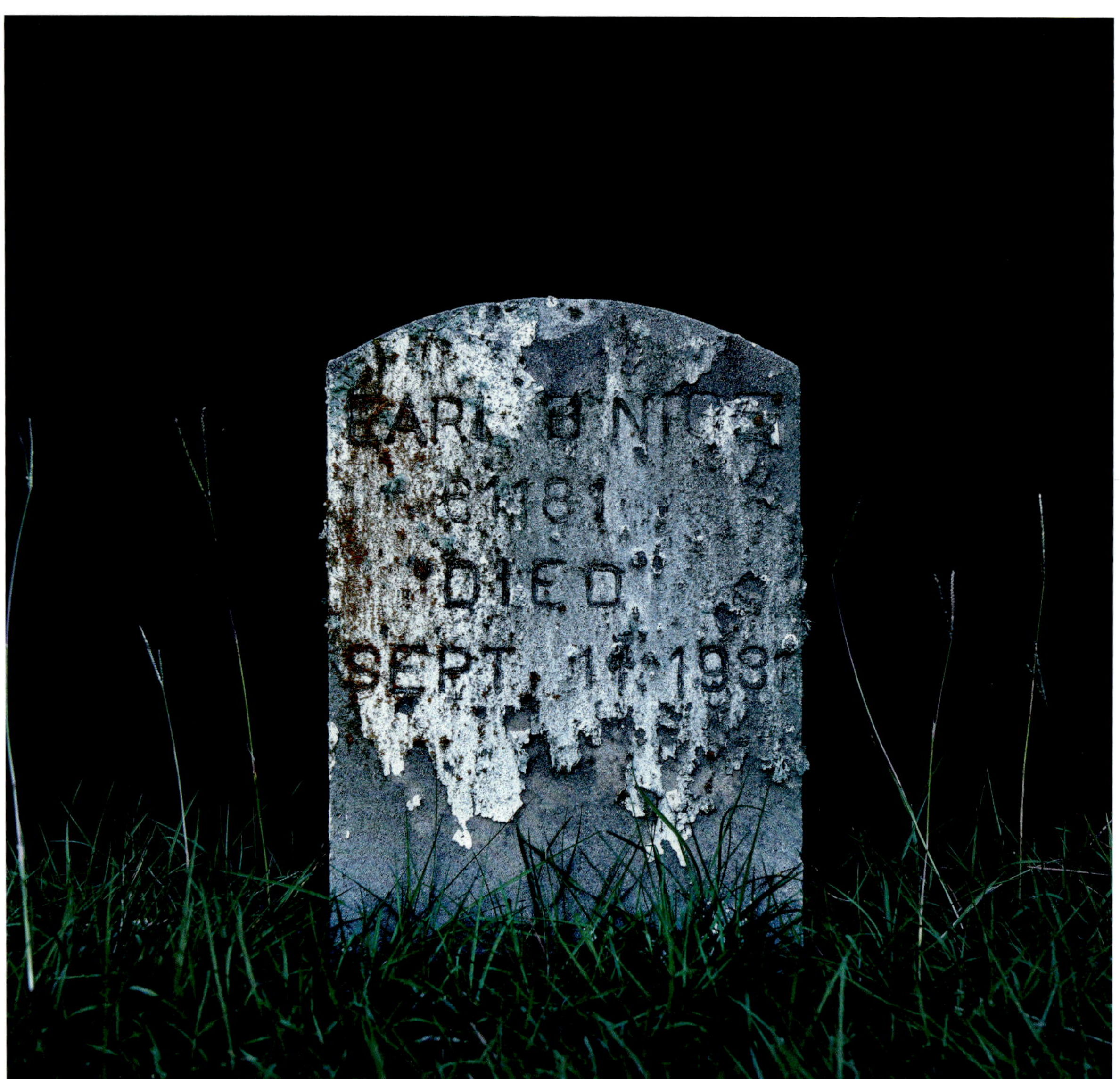

#080

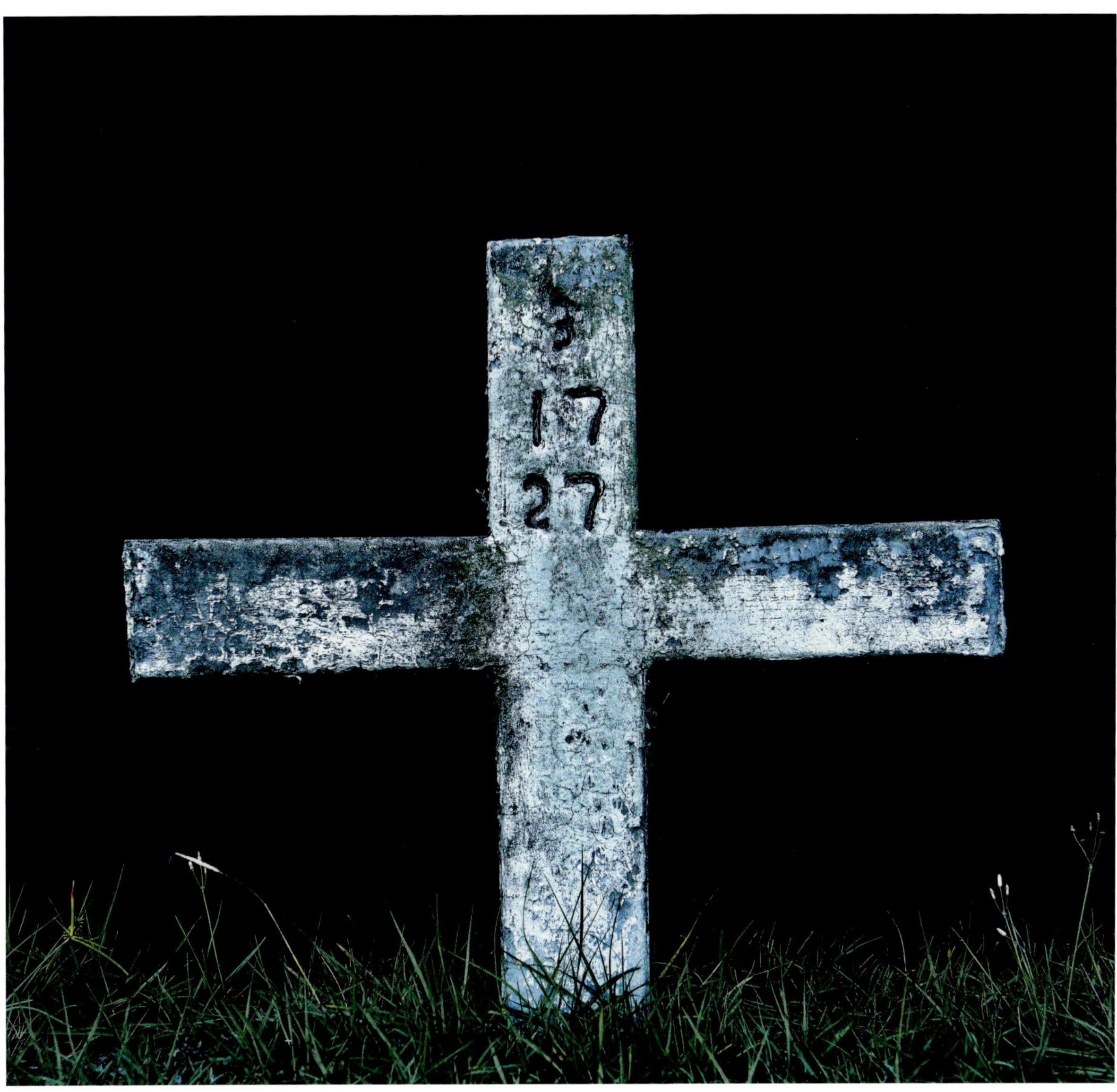

#169

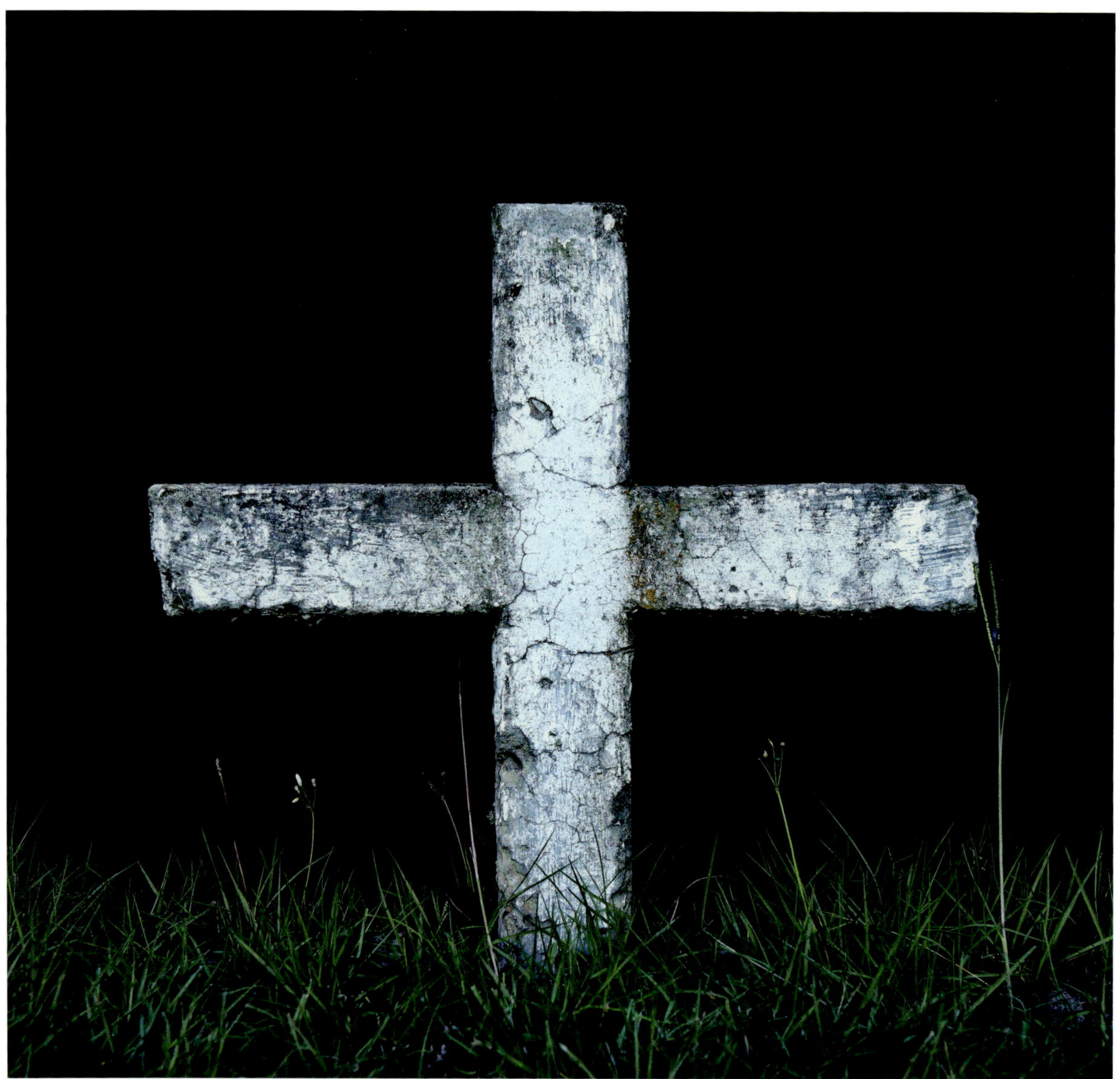

#173

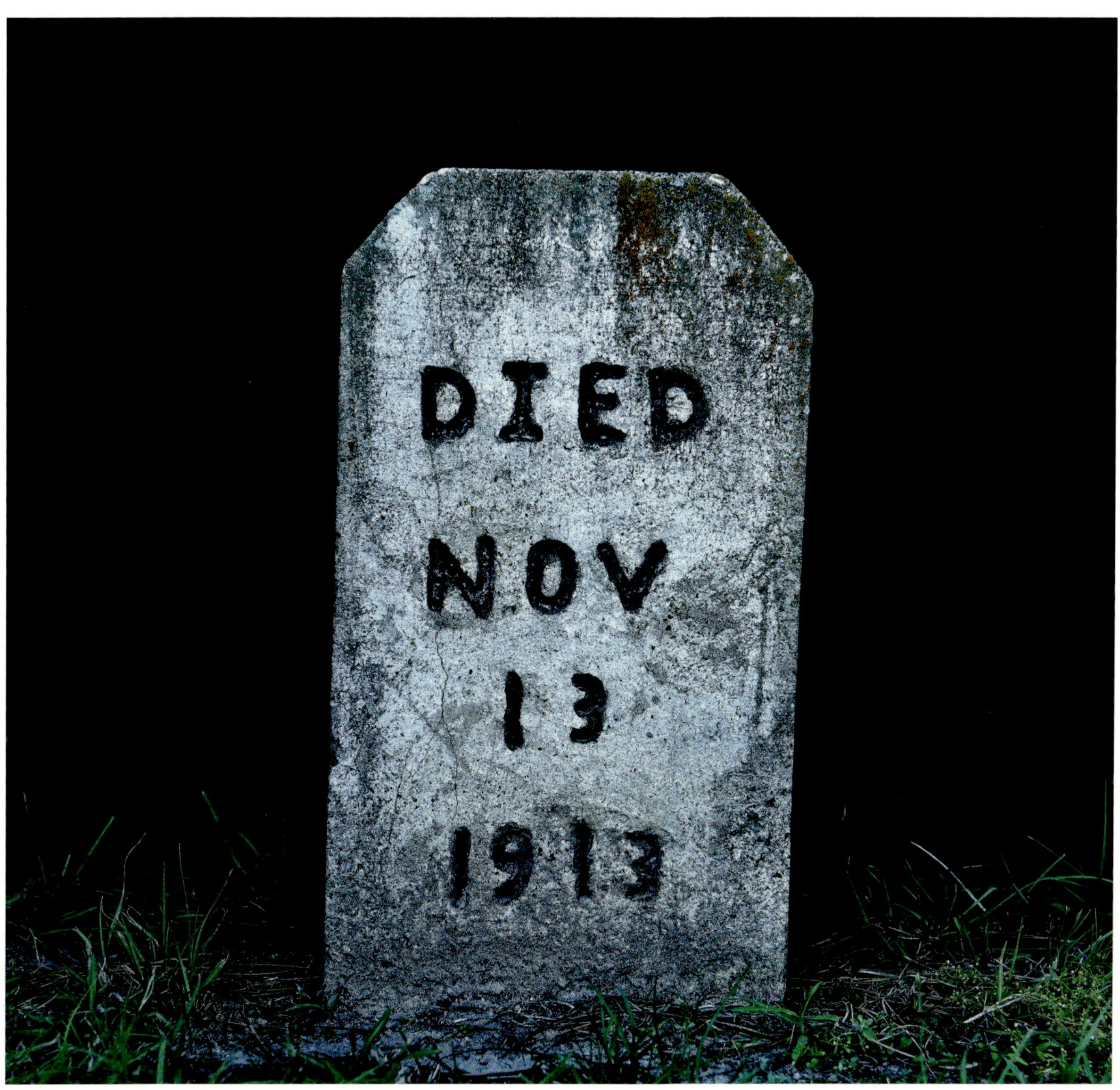

#145

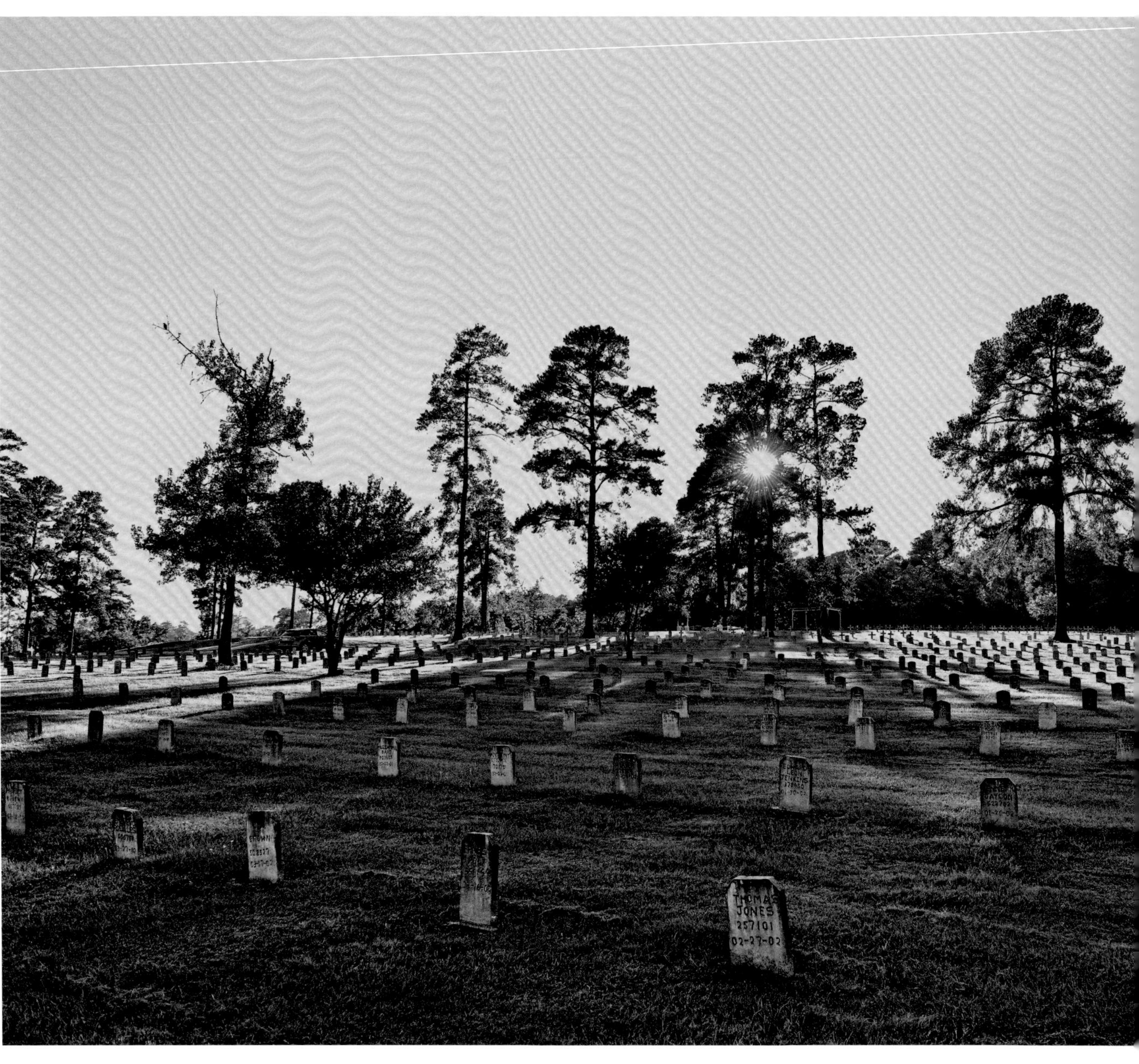

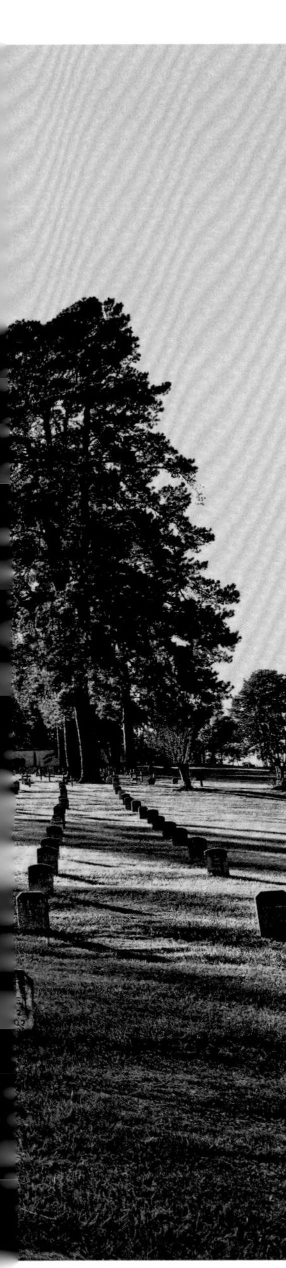

DISCLAIMER
Unfortunately, at times, information in the prisoner records and on grave markers do not match.

There are various reasons for these errors. One cause is the high turnover rate of prisoners assigned to cemetery maintenance resulting in a lack of continuity. A further problem is that at times prisoners serving as cemetery workers are given the task of recreating broken and illegible markers. These are not always checked by record-keeping personnel which results in an inconsequent standard for the inscriptions. For example, some markers show the burial date while others show the date of death.

A COMPREHENSIVE GUIDE TO THE GRAVE MARKERS

Page	Image no.	Name	Date of birth	Education level	Occupation	Crime
007	056	Edwin Rushing	January 1900			Murder
008	123	James Gunter	28 February 1965			Murder
009	092	Timothy Tyler Titsworth	8 March 1972	8 years	Roofer	Murder
010	094	Michael Wayne Hall	6 April 1979	9 years	Laborer	Murder
011	049	George Washington				Murder
012	116	Aua Lauti	18 June 1954	11 years	Landscaping	Murder
013	117	Michael Eugene Sharp	24 April 1954	13 years	Oilfield worker	Murder
014	113	Bruce E. Jorden	5 September 1918			Murder
015	101	Michael Harris	6 November 1962			Aggravated sexual assault
016	005	Francis Marion Snow	6 June 1878			Murder
017	030	Jay Kelly Pinkerton	14 February 1962	10 years	Truck driver	Murder
018	031	Joseph Blaine Starvaggi	November 1952		Cement finisher	Murder
019	040	Bishop Adams	1 January 1889	1 year		Murder
020	048	Edward Hart, Jr.	13 May 1917			Rape and robbery
021	054	Frank Noel	27 April 1902			Rape
022	062	Thomas Wayne Mason	31 December 1951	9 years	Drywaller	Murder
023	164	Victor Rogers	29 July 1959			
024	154	Raymond Minori	8 December 1941			Aggravated robbery
025	039	Donald White	7 December 1922			Rape
026	044	Reney Williams	7 November 1892		Auto mechanic	Rape
027	061	Tommy Ray Jackson	15 November 1956	14 years	Computer technician	Murder
028	026	Marvin Collier	29 December 1929	10 years		Robbery
029	070	Tony Lee Walker	15 April 1966	9 years	Welder	Murder
030	068	Ronford Lee Styron, Jr.	23 August 1969	11 years	Laborer	Murder
031	063	Jeffrey Henry Caldwel	1 March 1963	12 years	Commercial printer	Murder

Age at the time of crime	Sentence	Prison no.	Time on death row Time incarcerated	Date of death	Cause of death
25	Death	23	4 months	7 February 1924	Electric chair
22	Death	864	10 years	24 August 1997	Suicide by hanging
20	Death	999078	12 years	6 June 2006	Lethal injection
18	Death	999346	11 years	15 February 2011	Lethal injection
38	Death	2	5 months	8 February 1928	
31	Death	843	11 years	4 November 1997	Lethal injection
28	Death	740	14 years	19 November 1997	Lethal injection
25	Death	256	1 month	16 April 1944	Electric chair
44	10 years	1478915	1 year	19 August 2009	
49	Death	41	2 months	12 August 1927	Electric chair
17	Death	686	5 years	15 May 1986	Lethal injection
24	Death	586	12 years	10 September 1987	Lethal injection
41	Death	74	1 month	13 March 1930	Electric chair
25	Death	247	7 months	29 July 1942	Electric chair
23	Death	19	1 month	2 July 1925	Electric chair
39	Death	999035	8 years	12 June 2000	Lethal injection
		711240			Septic shock
57	20 years	787393	9 months	26 March 1998	Unknown
49	30 years	222292	11 years	12 January 1983	Unknown
38	Death	77	1 month	6 August 1930	Electric chair
27	Death	821	14 years	4 May 2000	Lethal injection
58	18 years	349737	5 years	14 June 1989	Unknown
26	Death	999082	8 years	10 September 2002	Lethal injection
24	Death	999124	7 years	16 May 2002	Lethal injection
25	Death	938	11 years	30 August 2000	Lethal injection

A COMPREHENSIVE GUIDE TO THE GRAVE MARKERS

Page	Image no.	Name	Date of birth	Education level	Occupation	Crime
032	136	Barney Lee				
033	066	Henry Lee Lucas	23 August 1936			Murder
034	067	Glen Mulder	9 June 1937			Attempted murder/ theft
035	148	Harle Humphreys	1905			Murder
036	177	Unidentified				
037	176	Unidentified				
038	076	Ronnie Hyde	21 October 1958	12 years	Laborer	Murder
039	171	Unidentified				
040	180	Salvador Betancourt	4 September 1953			Possession of heroin (habitual)
041	006	George Jefferson Hassell	July 1888			Murder
042	081	Antonio Garza	1901	9 years		Theft of a horse
043	093	Sean Derrick O'Brien	5 April 1975	9 years	Laborer	Murder
044	103	Robert Wayne Harris	28 February 1972	10 years	Laborer	Murder
045	015	Darryl Elroy Stewart	2 April 1955	12 years	Auto mechanic	Murder
046	168	Unidentified				
047	074	Roger Dale Vaughn	11 October 1954	10 years	Electrician	Murder
048	098	Christopher Jay Swift	12 February 1975	10 years	Laborer	Murder
049	106	Terry Lee Hankins	10 October 1974	9 years	Auto mechanic, laborer	Murder
050	114	Morgan Collan	14 April 1901			Murder
051	178	Unidentified				
052	125	Frederick Caldwell	29 November 1956			Aggravated robbery with deadly weapon
053	029	Elliot Rod Johnson	17 August 1958	9 years	Construction	Murder
054	057	Virgil Alvin Sims	18 December 1947			Possession of cocaine

Age at the time of crime	Sentence	Prison no.	Time on death row Time incarcerated	Date of death	Cause of death
		42515			
45	99 years	830114	16 years	2 March 2001	
40	99 years	310876	21 years	7 November 2001	
19	Death	10		22 May 1924	Execution
39	Death	999357	13 years	23 July 2013	Cellulitis (sp)
23	Life	273169	8 years	25 July 1984	Cardiopulmonary arrest
38	Death	837	1 month	10 February 1928	Electric chair
15	2 years	40470		30 September 1918	
18	Death	999131	12 years	11 July 2006	Lethal injection
28	Death	999364	12 years	20 September 2012	Lethal injection
24	Death	664	13 years	4 May 1993	Lethal injection
37	Death	999029	11 years	6 May 2003	Lethal injection
28	Death	999496	2 years	31 January 2007	Lethal injection
26	Death	99415	7 years	2 June 2009	Lethal injection
37	Death	205	2 months	19 August 1938	Electric chair
35	15 years	576166	4 years	1 January 1995	Cardiopulmonary arrest
24	Death	739		8 April 1982	Lethal injection
46	5 years	919285	5 years	25 May 2000	

A COMPREHENSIVE GUIDE TO THE GRAVE MARKERS

Page	Image no.	Name	Date of birth	Education level	Occupation	Crime
055	118	Raymond James Jones	1 January 1960	8 years	Laborer	Murder
056	102	Keith Steven Thurmond	31 October 1959	9 years	Master mechanic, air-conditioning technician, laborer	Murder
057	087	Arthur Danly	1895			Robbery by assault with a firearm
058	150	Unidentified	19 March 1917			
059	050	Ed Henderson				Rape
060	100	Michael F. Rosales	11 January 1974	10 years	Auto mechanic	Murder
061	022	Leon Royal	5 July 1937			Theft over 200 dollars (habitual)
062	099	Elkie Lee Taylor	14 December 1961	5 years	Laborer	Murder
063	142	James Demouchette	20 May 1955	9 years	Painter	Murder
064	133	Jimmy Jones	4 November 1940			Forgery by passing
065	021	Larry Smith	26 August 1955		Laborer	Murder
066	105	Santos Minjares	28 August 1971	9 years	Construction, laborer	Murder
067	017	Anthony Quinn Cook	4 January 1959	9 years	Construction	Murder
068	158	Hubert Glen Martz	12 November 1951			
069	075	Eddie Whitehead	16 May 1950		Auto mechanic	Driving while intoxicated
070	165	Christopher Whiteside	14 July 1948			Aggravated sexual assault of a child under 14
071	025	James Emery Paster	30 January 1945	12 years	Cook	Murder
072	112	Anthony Ray Westley	18 July 1960	8 years	Laborer	Murder
073	071	Rex Warren Mays	21 January 1960			Murder
074	073	Alva Curry	22 March 1969	9 years	Laborer	Murder
075	175	Unidentified				

Age at the time of crime	Sentence	Prison no.	Time on death row Time incarcerated	Date of death	Cause of death
28	Death	959	10 years	1 September 1999	Lethal injection
41	Death	999435	10 years	7 March 2012	Lethal injection
25	5 years	45084	1 month	27 September 1920	
		36964			
45	Death	12	1 month	9 June 1924	Electric chair
23	Death	999274	11 years	16 April 2009	Lethal injection
39	99 years	227019	12 years	11 April 1990	Renal disease
31	Death	999112	14 years	31 October 2008	Lethal injection
21	Death	572	15 years	22 September 1992	Lethal injection
46	25 years	463415	11 years	25 June 1998	AIDS/heart failure
22	Death	643	7 years	22 August 1986	Lethal injection
29	Death	999445	9 years	14 January 2012	Septic shock
29	Death	918	5 years	11 November 1993	Lethal injection
47	Death	641655	24 years	30 May 1994	Massive coronary
48	20 years	922152	3 years	18 July 2003	
47	99 years	744645	12 years	8 June 2008	
35	Death	752	5 years	20 September 1989	Lethal injection
23	Death	797	12 years	3 May 1997	Lethal injection
32	Death	999172	7 years	24 September 2002	Lethal injection
22	Death	999080	9 years	28 January 2003	Lethal injection

A COMPREHENSIVE GUIDE TO THE GRAVE MARKERS

Page	Image no.	Name	Date of birth	Education level	Occupation	Crime
076	153	Jesse Casso	18 April 1947			Possession of cocaine
077	007	Emma Lawton	1894			Burglary
078	166	Timothy Athey	18 October 1971			Aggravated sexual assault of a child under 17
079	085	Yuimio Garcia	1899			Robbery by use of a firearm
080	120	Albert Ables				
081	159	Tara Acosta	1 April 1964			Theft
082	091	Jesse March	1899			Assault with intent to murder
083	109	Dorsie Johnson, Jr.	10 March 1967	11 years	Janitor	Murder
084	019	Justin Lee May	26 April 1946	11 years	Welder	Murder
085	078	Henry Helms	3 February 1896			Murder
086	018	Curtis Lee Johnson	1954	7 years		Murder
087	137	Torres Santos				
088	138	J. F. Crosley	10 September 1902			
089	095	Larry Donell Davis	9 October 1967	9 years	Laborer	Murder
090	167	Unidentified				
091	043	Joe Nathan				
092	033	Herman Robert Charles Clark, Jr.	26 July 1946	14 years	Auto mechanic	Murder
093	108	Robert Excell White	14 March 1938	10 years	Auto mechanic	Murder
094	080	Earl Bonfoe	4 May 1895			Forgery
095	169	Unidentified				
096	173	Unidentified				
097	145	Unidentified				

Age at the time of crime	Sentence	Prison no.	Time on death row Time incarcerated	Date of death	Cause of death
37	20 years	384686	15 years	22 March 1999	Liver disease
24	2 years	42391	9 months	20 December 1918	
25	10 years	1105396	5 years	28 May 2008	
18	5 years	41282	2 years	7 May 1919	
		185097		20 April 1954	
27	20 years	618273	6 years	4 September 1998	Acute pancreatitis/hepatitis
17		40131	2 months	28 April 1918	
19	Death	850	11 years	4 June 1997	Lethal injection
32	Death	783	14 years	7 May 1992	Lethal injection
33	Death	70	1 month	6 September 1929	Electric chair
29	Death	761	9 years	11 August 1992	Lethal injection
27	Death	999316	9 years	31 July 2008	Lethal injection
				13 July 1930	Pneumonia
34	Death	715	12 years	16 December 1994	Lethal injection
36	Death	511	25 years	30 March 1999	Lethal injection
16	3 years	61181	5 months	11 September 1911	

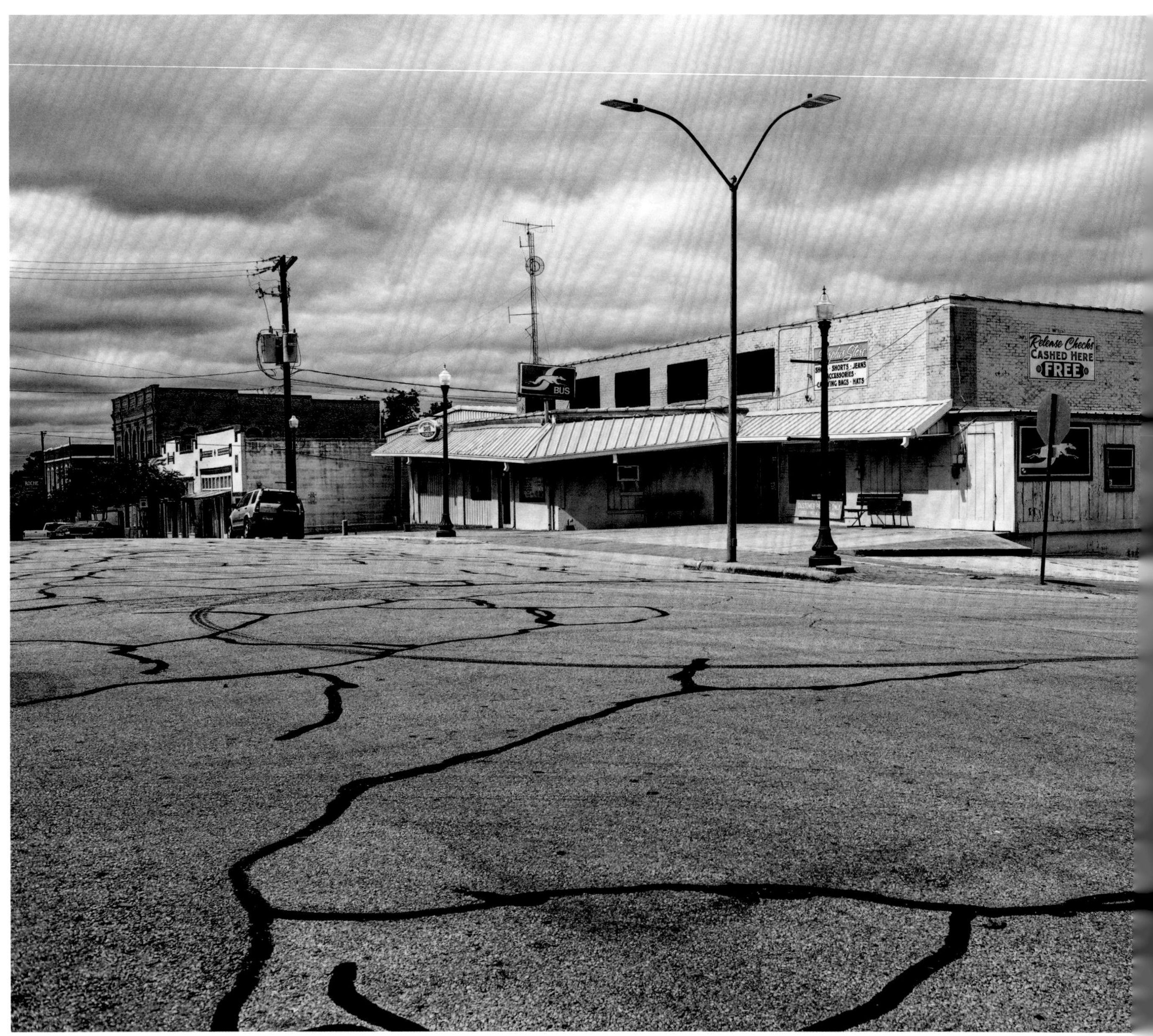
BUS
SHORTS · JEANS
ACCESSORIES
CARRYING BAGS · HATS
Release Checks
CASHED HERE
FREE

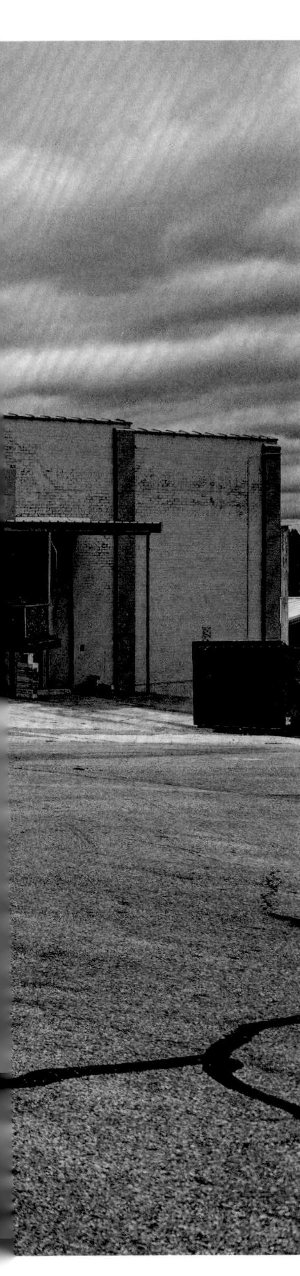

HOW IT STARTED

Fascinated by life and death in a country that seems to value both freedom and "civilized" destruction, I stumbled upon the town of Huntsville, Texas, USA. A long series of binge Googlings led me to Peckerwood Hill, also known as Captain Joe Byrd Cemetery, where I found hundreds of gravestones under which lay the unclaimed bodies of convicted criminals from the Texas state prison system.

In 2010, I packed my camera and left Sweden for Texas. What I found there caught me completely off guard: a burial ground of unclaimed deceased prisoners which filled me with an eerie sense of unease. So much so, in fact, that I could not stay in Huntsville that night, but instead drove 70 miles to a hotel in Houston before returning the next day. I took a few photographs before deciding I couldn't complete the project on my own and returned to Sweden. Two years later, I began discussing making a photographic portrait of the cemetery with renowned photographer Håkan Ludwigson. In 2013, we headed to the United States, spending a week photographing Peckerwood Hill and dining with prison guards in trailer parks, discussing life, death and the Texas state penal system.

The images captured were taken during the day using a black backdrop. Some of the most visually interesting headstones at the cemetery had lost their engraving entirely, while one of my favorite crosses contained fragments of text, though not enough to identify the inmate it memorialized.

Lennart Grebelius

LENNART GREBELIUS

Lennart Grebelius is a Swedish artist whose early fascination with the human condition, mathematics and science led him to examine methods of turning abstract ideas into tangible objects. His pioneering works in the field include: *20 Billion Years* (2003), *Who Am I?* (2007), *One Trillion Digits of Pi* (2016) and *The Divine Proportion* (2012).

Since the early 1990s, Grebelius has explored the concept of death and killing in Western civilization, specifically in the USA where the taking of a human life is still legal in many states. Among his works on this subject are facsimiles of final meal requests (*Final Meal Requests,* 2013), manuals intended for executioners (*Electrocution Equipment and Manual,* 2012) and chronological reports from executions (*On the Death of Alton Coleman,* 2011).

HÅKAN LUDWIGSON

Håkan Ludwigson is an internationally renowned Swedish photographer. For 50 years, he has been carrying out commercial assignments while also roaming the world for the American travel magazine *Condé Nast Traveler.*

Throughout his career, Håkan has always dedicated time to personal projects. He is now in a position where he can focus even more on this area and also manage his vast archive.

Håkan has produced two books: *Taken out of Context* (2006) and *Balls and Bulldust* (2015). His photographs have been shown in numerous exhibitions and are sought after among collectors. He has won a number of international awards from institutions such as the *Art Directors Club,* Miami, the *D&AD Awards,* London, *The One Show,* New York, and a *Silver Lion,* Cannes.

Consulting editor:
Nadine Barth

Project management:
Constanze Korb, Hatje Cantz

Copy editing:
Andrea Cavegn

Graphic design and typesetting:
Håkan Ludwigson & Andrew Cowie

Final art:
Alexandra Augustsson

Typeface:
Berthold Akzidenz, PT Serif, Courier

Paper:
Profimatt, 200 g/m²

Production:
Heidrun Zimmermann, Hatje Cantz

Printing, binding and reproductions:
DZA Druckerei zu Altenburg GmbH,
Altenburg

© 2019 Hatje Cantz Verlag, Berlin,
and Lennart Grebelius

© 2019 for the reproduced works by
Håkan Ludwigson: the artist

Published by
Hatje Cantz Verlag GmbH
Mommsenstraße 27
10629 Berlin
Tel. +49 30 3464678-00
Fax +49 30 3464678-29
www.hatjecantz.de
A Ganske Publishing Group company

Hatje Cantz books are available internationally
at selected bookstores. For more information
about our distribution partners, please visit
our website at www.hatjecantz.com.

ISBN 978-3-7757-4546-8

Printed in Germany

A special thank-you to Ted Tadlock, a staff member at Sam Houston State University, for his
invaluable assistance. Ted catalogs graves at Captain Joe Byrd Cemetery and he has assisted
in the detective work of confirming the information on the graves.